# The FIGHT for PEACE

**N**o one can be a pacifist
without being ready
to fight for peace
and die for peace.

~Mary Heaton Vorse,
*Labor journalist and world peace activist, 1935*

# The FIGHT for PEACE

## A HISTORY OF ANTIWAR MOVEMENTS IN AMERICA

TED GOTTFRIED

TWENTY-FIRST CENTURY BOOKS · MINNEAPOLIS

*For Harriet and all the other Peace People*

Twenty-First Century Books
A division of Lerner Publishing Group
241 First Avenue North
Minneapolis, Minnesota 55401 U.S.A.

Website address: www.lernerbooks.com

Author's acknowledgments
I am grateful to personnel of the New York Central Research Library and the Mid-Manhattan Library, as well as Moveon.org for aid in gathering material for this book. Also, my appreciation for research help from Rudy Kornmann and Dick Josephs, who provided an alternative perspective to this subject. Thanks, as always, to my wife, Harriet, whose comments and advice on this text were invaluable.


Library of Congress Cataloging-in-Publication Data

Gottfried, Ted.
     The fight for peace : a history of antiwar movements in America / by Ted Gottfried.
        p.   cm. — (People's history)
     Includes bibliographical references and index.
     ISBN-13: 978–0–7613–2932–9 (lib. bdg. : alk. paper)
     ISBN-10: 0–7613–2932–3 (lib. bdg. : alk. paper)
     1. Peace movements—United States—History. I. Title.
JZ5584.U6G685 2006
303.6'6—dc22                                 2005005758

Manufactured in the United States of America
1 2 3 4 5 6 – JR – 11 10 09 08 07 06

# CONTENTS

**N**o Blood for Oil!
—*antiwar chant, 2000*

# PREFACE

**A** small group of approximately seventy-five mostly middle-aged and middle-class people gathered on a village green in Stratford, Connecticut, in the early evening of March 16, 2003. It was a balmy spring evening, one of the first to follow an extremely harsh winter. There was a full moon overhead. The group formed a loose circle, widening it for newcomers as they arrived. They lit candles, inserting them in plastic cups to catch the melting wax. Above the flickering candles, their faces were solemn. They had come together in a vigil to protest going to war against Iraq.

A Unitarian minister spoke briefly, her words a message of peace. There was silence. A man stepped forward and sang an antiwar song he had composed. A woman spoke. Another man sang. The group was silent for long moments, solemn, meditative.

From the shadows behind the group, a loud voice suddenly shattered the silence and told the gatherers they should be ashamed of themselves. There followed a tirade accusing the group of un-Americanism, of being traitors to their country, of not supporting the soldiers fighting to preserve their freedom, and, finally, of being Communists. The speaker was alone, unsupported, his anger conveying a certain courage as he confronted the group. A young man, roughly the same age as the one who had interrupted the proceedings, detached himself from the group and went over to him. They talked softly, one-on-one, to what resolution the other members of the group couldn't tell.

A last song of peace was sung. The candles were extinguished. The group dispersed. Behind them the question hung in the air. In opting for peace in a time of war, were they being disloyal to their country? Was their dissent treason? At what point did opposition to war become aid to the enemy?

Four days later, U.S. forces attacked in Iraq. The war was being waged. The questions remained. They were the same questions American antiwar proponents had faced since before the American Revolution (1775–1783).

# REVOLUTION AND PACIFISM

**O**n March 3, 2003, as part of an organized protest against preparations for a U.S.-led war in Iraq, antiwar protesters staged more than one thousand readings of the ancient Greek play *Lysistrata*. The readings took place in fifty-nine countries, including China, Egypt, Israel, Norway, Argentina, Pakistan, and the United States. The play describes how an Athenian woman ends the Second Peloponnesian War by organizing all the Greek wives to stop making love to their husbands as long as the fighting lasts. Written by Aristophanes in 411 B.C., *Lysistrata* is one of the first examples of antiwar discourse in western society.

In eastern society, in sixth-century B.C. China, following the teachings of the philosopher Lao-tzu, Taoists embraced *wu-wei* (literally, nonaction), which stressed inner peace over physical violence. In India during the same period, Buddhists adopted ahimsa (noninjury), a philosophy of passive resistance for countering violence. Centuries later, Mohandas K. Gandhi would interpret ahimsa as nonviolent protest to do away with repression in the face of government violence. Still later, in the United States, Dr. Martin Luther King Jr. would forge a civil rights movement based on Gandhi's example, a path also followed by Nelson Mandela in South Africa. Nonviolent protest and civil disobedience would be techniques used by antiwar movements around the world.

## ANTIWAR CHRISTIANITY

For Christians, devotion to peace had also been part of Jesus' teaching. Always he had advised his followers to turn the other cheek and forgo violence. However, the first actual peace movement in western civilization wasn't launched until the tenth century A.D. At that time, Europe was little more than a collection of nation-states bent on plundering one another. Some of this occurred under the guise of government. Much of it was simply a matter of regional bands of armed soldiers raiding other regions and being raided in return. The only stable element in what was frequently a chaotic world was the Christian church of that time.

In A.D. 989, the church held a council at Charroux in France. Its purpose was to abolish violence and warfare and to guarantee safe passage for religious pilgrims and other travelers. The council declared the Peace of God, a set of religious edicts. The edicts banned the entering of churches by force and forbade the plundering of holy institutions. The Peace of God said property could not be seized from peasants and upheld the rights of noncombatants to refuse to fight in a conflict. As an afterthought, protection of merchants and their property was added to the decrees of the Peace of God.

Almost forty years later, in 1027, the Peace of God was amended to include the Truce of God. This provided for "periodic armistices between feuding parties, suspending private wars from Wednesday night to Monday morning." Associations of peacekeepers were sworn in to enforce the Truce of God. Those who violated it faced both spiritual and physical punishment.

Although the Truce of God continued to be pursued throughout the eleventh century, it was not very effective. The problem of continued carnage in Europe was the main topic at the Council of Clermont held in 1095. It was decided that to spare Europe, the feuding nobility and their bands of soldiers would enlist in a great Crusade to rescue the Holy Land from the non-Christian "infidels." In this way, the peace

*The Crusades were a series of military expeditions organized in the name of Christianity during the Middle Ages, ostensibly to recapture Palestine.*

movement removed much of the violence and anarchy from Europe and redirected them to the more profitable plunder of Islamic lands.

## THE SOCIETY OF FRIENDS

Nonviolent movements in European Christianity may not have been very effective over the succeeding centuries, but they prevailed. The religion split into denominations and sects, and some of these subgroups held a strict antiwar doctrine as the core of their belief. In many seventeenth- and eighteenth-century countries—The Netherlands, Germany, and Britain in particular—antiwar congregations endured rejection and persecution. To escape, many religious peace groups emigrated to the colonies of the New World.

Among the first to come to America were the Quakers, also known as the Society of Friends. They had embraced the words of Jesus and had adopted a doctrine of living as peacemakers. Toward the end of the seventeenth century, Friends began settling in the Massachusetts Bay Colony, Rhode Island, Maryland, Virginia, and North Carolina. In 1681 Quaker leader William Penn obtained a charter from King Charles II of England to set up an experiment for an American colony to be governed by Quaker principles of pacifism and religious tolerance. The result was Pennsylvania, where the Quakers were a controlling majority until the mid-eighteenth century, when they were outnumbered by an influx of settlers of other denominations. After the Friends refused to vote funds for the French and Indian War, their influence in Pennsylvania politics declined. Throughout the colonies, between 1758 and 1800, Quakers emancipated all their slaves. When Stephen Hopkins, nine times governor of Rhode Island, refused to free his one slave, the Quaker congregation to which he belonged disowned him.

A similar fate befell Nathanael Greene but for a very different reason. Greene was one of nine children of a devout Rhode Island Quaker family. On July 20, 1774, he married nineteen-year-old

*Discredited as a Quaker because he chose to fight in the American Revolution, General Nathanael Greene was considered second only to George Washington as a military strategist.*

Catharine Littlefield, also a Quaker. In October 1774, Greene became convinced that Britain was treating the American colonies unjustly and that the colonies were facing war. Despite his Quaker background, he helped organize a militia. He was informed that he was no longer welcome as a member of the Society of Friends to which he had belonged since birth.

Because he had a slightly crippled leg, Greene could not be an officer in the militia he had organized, so he enlisted as a private. However, after the American Revolution actually began, Greene became brigadier general of the Rhode Island Army. Eventually General Washington's second-in-command of the American forces, he was twice offered the post of secretary of war after the Revolution and twice refused it.

# THE "FREE QUAKERS"

Greene was not the only Quaker to put patriotism before pacifism. Some Quakers felt strongly that the call to arms against the British required them to set aside their peace doctrines for the duration of the struggle. In Philadelphia they called themselves Free Quakers and organized troops of militia to fight alongside Washington's Continental Army. The majority of Pennsylvania Friends, however, clung to their pacifist beliefs and disowned those Friends who joined the military. The Free Quakers reacted. They responded that although the peace Quakers had "separated yourselves from us, and declared that you have no unity with us," they could not withhold Free Quakers' rights to the property that members of Friends societies held in common.

Although the pacifist Quakers refused to take part in the conflict, that did not stop them from having strong views in favor of one side or the other. Some Quakers believed in the cause of the Revolution, and some remained loyal to the British crown. War brought hard times and labor shortages as men went off to war, and Quakers had to scratch out their living as best they could. Pacifist Quakers sympathetic to the American cause nevertheless sold food and supplies to the British. In Chester County, Pennsylvania, one prominent Quaker guided an invading British force through defenses set up by his neighbors.

This was not typical. Most Quakers simply struggled to stay withdrawn from the struggle. In some cases, they were able to do this to an extent because local counties worked out arrangements where they could perform community services without violating their pacifist ideals. Friends served in hospitals and performed other humanist jobs as a substitute for providing money for the war or serving in the army. They were required to satisfy the Pennsylvania Test Act, which required all citizens to swear loyalty to the 1776 Pennsylvania Constitution. In some counties sympathetic to Quakers, however, they were allowed to avoid the Militia Law, which would have required them to fight with county troops or to pay a fine that went to support the war effort.

Nevertheless, Quakers were often regarded as traitors and collaborators by their non-Quaker neighbors. Quakers were beaten by civilian patriots. Their property was seized. They were robbed at gunpoint. They faced public censure, harassment, and punishment from public officials. They were not the only pacifists in colonial America to suffer for their convictions.

## THE BRETHREN

Another persecuted pacifist denomination was the Brethren, also known as Dunkards because of their practice of three immersions during baptism. The sect had originated in 1708 in Germany and eventually had spread to parts of Switzerland and Denmark. Members of the Brethren adhered to a strict doctrine of nonresistance and opposition to military service. On many occasions, this stance had caused them to be jailed.

Always a minority and persecuted in many places, they finally migrated in large numbers to Pennsylvania and New Jersey. By 1776 twenty-eight congregations of Brethren were living in the colonies along the Atlantic seacoast. Their total membership was around five thousand (a large number for such a minor denomination in those times). With the advent of the American Revolution, they were once again caught between pacifism and persecution.

Some of the Brethren tended toward loyalty to the British crown because they had found freedoms in colonial America that they had not been able to enjoy back in Europe. Nevertheless, they would not fight for the British. Nor would they move away from pacifism as the Free Quakers had. However, by removing themselves as completely as possible from the war, they also removed themselves from their neighbors and the surrounding communities. This was resented. Their attitude aroused suspicion. Many Brethren communities fell victim to mob violence. The American revolutionary government took action to confiscate Brethren property. As a result, the Brethren became even more withdrawn. This pattern of isolation is still more or less adhered to by the roughly 266,000 Brethren in the United States.

## THE MENNONITES

The Brethren and the Quakers are two of the three historic peace denominations in the United States. The third is the Mennonites. Their founder, the Dutch priest Menno Simons, defined their core belief in support of peace. "The regenerated do not go to war nor engage in strife," he said. "They are the children of peace who have beaten their swords into plowshares and their spears into pruning hooks and know of no war."

Because they had a long tradition of highly skilled craftsmanship, Mennonites were valued by their rulers in Germany, the Netherlands, Switzerland, and other parts of Europe. The rulers tolerated the Mennonites' refusal to serve in various military forces. Nevertheless, they were sometimes persecuted for their antimilitary principles. From the late seventeenth century and throughout the eighteenth century, groups of Mennonites migrated to America.

Like the Brethren, they kept to themselves. They formed small farming communities, many in Pennsylvania, and spoke only German. This was regarded as a way of preserving their traditions and their antiwar identity.

On the brink of the American Revolution, the Mennonite minister Benjamin Hershey sent the following petition defining the Menno-nite position to the Pennsylvania Assembly: "It is our principle to feed the hungry and give the thirsty drink; we have dedicated ourselves to serve all men in everything that can be helpful to the preservation of men's lives, but we find no freedom in giving, or doing, or assisting in anything by which men's lives are destroyed or hurt."

*Tar and feathering was a brutal and common punishment in colonial America. The hot tar was as painful going on the skin as it was being taken off after it cooled.*

As the war continued, however, the Mennonite position attracted more and more resentment from those whose sons and brothers were doing the fighting against the British. Along with Quakers and Brethren, in some parts of the country, Mennonites were actively persecuted for their refusal to participate in the war effort. Tar and feathering was common. This involved pouring hot pine tar with chicken feathers embedded in it over a victim who was then paraded around town as a means of humiliation.

Many Mennonites fled to Canada to escape the war. Since British Loyalists were doing the same, American patriots made little distinction between the two groups. Both were regarded as traitors. Mennonites in Lancaster County, Pennsylvania, didn't flee. However, in 1783 they were charged with treason for feeding retreating British soldiers.

The Mennonites, like the Quakers and the Brethren, still act on their antiwar convictions. In recent times, they have been active in protesting the Vietnam War (1957–1975), the Gulf War (1991), and the latest ongoing war in Iraq (2003). They continue to believe in "love as the central directing element in all relationships, including a concern for human need and the enemy; rejection of violence, military service and war."

# THE WAR OF 1812

The many wars that took place in the newly formed United States between Native Americans and U.S. military forces from 1783 to the War of 1812 (1812–1815) have been lost in the shrouds of history. Lands were sold by tribes that had no clear ownership of them, and treaties were breached by a succession of politicians spurred on by land developers. Native tribes and U.S. forces conducted brutal raids in which men, women, and children were slaughtered. A bitter savagery marked the period.

Quakers were notable exceptions to this savagery. The Quaker leader William Penn had signed a peace treaty with Tammany, leader of the Delaware tribe. Additional treaties between Quakers and other tribes followed. None was ever violated. All lived up to the letter Penn sent to Indians expressing his "great love and regard for them" and his eagerness to share with them "a kind, just and peaceable life."

This attitude often earned Quakers great hostility from their white neighbors during the years leading up to the War of 1812. Quaker men refused to participate in raids on tribal villages. They met with Native Americans in an effort to prevent violence and even warned them of attacks. These Quakers were regarded as traitors to their race, to their region, and to their country. Treason was charged against Quakers because of the widespread belief that the tribes were being armed and incited by the British. There was some truth to this.

## THE BATTLE OF TIPPECANOE

According to Professor Howard Zinn, "In the Revolutionary War almost every important Indian nation fought on the side of the British." During the years that followed, American settlers pushed their way into tribal lands in the South and West. By 1800 about seven hundred thousand white settlers had spread out over Ohio, Indiana, Illinois, Alabama, and Mississippi. They outnumbered Native Americans eight to one. "Between 1795 and 1809 the Indians parted with some 48 million acres," reports historian Samuel Eliot Morison. He writes that, "although the Indians faithfully fulfilled their treaty stipulations, white pioneers in the Northwest committed the most wanton and cruel murders of them."

The Native Americans formed a tribal league to fight back. They obtained rifles from the British troops in Canada. They were led by the Shawnee chief Tecumseh.

However, Tecumseh was absent on November 7, 1811, when the governor of the Indiana Territory, William Henry Harrison, led an armed raid on the village that served as the tribal league's

*The Battle of Tippecanoe in 1811 is remembered as an extremely bloody confrontation in which the death toll was high on both sides.*

headquarters. The troops killed not only the warriors but Native American women and children as well.

Hailed as a great victory by the Americans, the Battle of Tippecanoe, as it was called, confirmed the suspicion that the Native Americans were using weapons provided by the British. It became widely believed that the British had sponsored Tecumseh's tribal league. This was corroborated when it was learned that, following the Battle of Tippecanoe, Tecumseh met with British governor general Sir George Prevost in Canada.

## MANIFEST DESTINY

The spreading out of the United States over tribal lands was necessary to fulfill Manifest Destiny. The slogan, fast becoming government policy, envisioned the United States controlling the entire North American continent. This would prevent colonialization by European powers that might compete for the continent's considerable natural resources.

Acquiring Native American land, either by purchase or seizure, did not, by itself, satisfy the policy of Manifest Destiny. Our neighbors on the continent, Canada and Mexico, also had valuable lands. Incited by an alliance between the British based in Canada and the Native American tribes, U.S. citizens began calling for military action to seize Canada. The attitude is summed up by historian-author Peter M. Rinaldo in his book *Unnecessary Wars:* "A conquest of Canada would not only secure more land but also eliminate the base for Indian attacks. A bonus would be to take over the rich fur trade that the Canadians enjoyed with the Indians."

Opposition to a war to conquer Canada by the Society of Friends and other peace groups was no more effective than whistling in the wind. A different factor was going to both fuel the demand for war, and—surprisingly—provide the impetus for one of the strongest anti-war movements in U.S. history. This was the impressment of American merchant seamen by the British Royal Navy.

## THE *CHESAPEAKE* INCIDENT

Impressment was the forcible seizure of sailors from U.S. merchant ships to serve in the British navy. British crews were made up of men rounded up from the waterfronts of Britain and forced to serve aboard warships. They were paid poorly, and conditions were miserable. Food was often spoiled and rations were small. Disease aboard ships was common and mostly went untreated. Many of these shanghaied sailors were killed or injured in battle. Whenever they reached port, many British sailors deserted and signed on with American merchant ships, which offered decent pay and far better working conditions. The large number of such desertions became a major problem for the British.

The British began stopping and searching U.S. merchant vessels in order to recapture "deserters." Some American ships refused to be boarded. On June 22, 1807, when the U.S. frigate *Chesapeake* ignored a boarding order from the British warship *Leopard,* the British opened fire. Three *Chesapeake* men were killed and eighteen wounded. When news of the incident reached the United States, there was a public outcry for war against Britain.

To avoid such a war, President Thomas Jefferson persuaded Congress to pass the Embargo Act of 1807. It forbid U.S. ships to sail from American ports to foreign destinations. This prevented the vessels' being harassed by the British, but it also hurt American shipping and export traders. Those most affected were the merchants of New England, who lost eight million dollars over the following fifteen months. They had

*British troops forcibly remove "deserters" from the* Chesapeake *in the early 1800s.*

led the outcry against the impressment of American seamen, but they began complaining that the Embargo Act was far more harmful to American trade than the searching of merchant ships had been. As a result, the Embargo Act was repealed on March 1, 1809.

## THE WAR HAWKS

The British navy continued to stop and search American merchant ships. Claiming that American sailors' papers were forged, they impressed them into British service. Between 1800 and the start of the War of 1812, as many as six thousand Americans were abducted.

In Congress a group of roughly twenty representatives from the South and West clamored for a declaration of war against Britain. Known as the war hawks, they were led by Henry Clay of Kentucky and John C. Calhoun of South Carolina. Most of the press in the South and West backed their cause. Typical was the February 12, 1812, article in the Circleville, Ohio, *Fredonian* calling for "the conquest of Canada." Another goal of the war hawks was to seize Florida from Britain's ally, Spain.

During this prelude to war, "northern shipowners, upon whom the [impressment] losses fell with special weight, did not ask for armed intervention. On the contrary, they took great pains to prove that the federal government's report listing thousands of impressment outrages was false, and they were almost unanimous in their opposition to drawing the sword against England." They believed that once war broke out, the effect on American trade would be disastrous. Most northern politicians were antiwar doves.

## WAR IS DECLARED

On June 1, 1812, President James Madison, under heavy pressure from the war hawks, requested that the Twelfth Congress of the United States consider declaring war on Britain. Madison pointed out that war "is a solemn question which the Constitution wisely confides to the legislative department of the government." In effect, Madison was reaffirming the clause in the Constitution that gives war-making powers to Congress, rather than to the president. (Antiwar advocates would raise this same issue during the Vietnam War and again during the 2003 invasion of Iraq.)

The House of Representatives met secretly. The war hawks were afraid antiwar advocates would stir up opposition to war. On June 4, they passed a declaration of war by a vote of 79 to 49, indicating significant opposition to the measure. The Senate debated for twelve days, finally passing the measure by 19 to 13. On June 18, 1812, the United States declared war against Great Britain.

New England opposition was immediate. The governors of Massachusetts and Connecticut refused to allocate forces to man the all-important Atlantic coastal defenses. Bankers in New England continued to lend money to Britain but refused to lend money to the U.S. government. In Vermont and upstate New York, farmers sold crucial supplies—not just food and cloth, but on occasion gunpowder—to the British army in Canada. In New York City and Philadelphia, antiwar sentiment mounted when the British blockaded the two cities' harbors. This move prevented merchant vessels from sailing into or out of the ports and resulted in driving many of the businesses in those cities into bankruptcy.

## FOR PEACE AND PROFIT

New Englanders protested that the war was being fought to fulfill the war hawks' plans to expand U.S. territory northward into Canada. Although this was true, "ambitious plans to invade Canada were never realized." U.S. forces did raid York (modern Toronto, Ontario) and burn down the Parliament buildings. The British retaliated by burning and sacking Washington, D.C. The Battle of Canada, however, was fought mainly in the U.S. Congress rather than in the vast wilderness the war hawks coveted.

Congress's antiwar forces, calling themselves the Quids, confronted the war hawks. Their leader, oddly enough, was not a northerner, but John Randolph of Virginia, a state where majority sentiment supported expansion into both Canada and Native American territories. Maverick Randolph was an acid-tongued debater whose demeanor was as striking as his crackling responses to the war hawks. He would stride into the chamber when Congress was in session dressed in forest-hued Virginia riding clothes, preceded by sometimes yipping hunting dogs who were seemingly unintimidated by the snap of the whip meant to control them. "Agrarian cupidity [rural self-interest]!" he would roar, summing up the reasons behind the war. He insisted that "one word—like the whip-poor-will, but one monotonous tone—Canada! Canada! Canada!" was what the hawks were after.

Dramatic as Randolph's arguments were, they were no match for the patriotic fervor stirred up by the war hawks. New England may have been against the war, but the rest of the country, except for a

*John Randolph's fiery rhetoric and occasionally bizarre behavior probably did his pacifist cause more harm than good. He was eventually declared insane.*

few antiwar religionists like the Quakers and the Unitarians, were out for British blood. Still, as the war proceeded, with no decisive victory on either side, antiwar sentiment in New England mounted.

One reason for this was a change in the way the British enforced the blockade against New England ports. Throughout much of the war, eager to encourage New England antiwar sentiment, the British blockade had turned a blind eye to imports of iron and steel destined for ports in Massachusetts and Rhode Island. Yankee importers grew wealthy selling these products to the quartermaster of the U.S. Army, in which their sons refused to serve. However, toward the end of the war, the British strictly enforced the blockade of these ports, determined to deny the Americans goods used for making war. Forced to tighten their belts, New Englanders became increasingly eager for peace.

## SECESSION: "THIS MAD PROJECT"

By the spring of 1814, leaders in New England were talking about separating from the Union. In December, even as negotiations were under way to end the war, arrangements were made for a secret meeting to discuss the impact of "Mr. Madison's War" on the economies of various northern states, as well as the possibility of secession. What followed was the Hartford Convention, which John Quincy Adams called "this mad project of national suicide."

The most eager secessionists at the Hartford Convention were the importers who had profited most by the war. They were resolved "to dissolve . . . their union" with the United States. Moderates prevailed over them, however, and the question of secession was shelved. One demand that was agreed on was a measure that "would deprive the slavocracy of representation in Congress based on the Negro population." As things stood, each slave held in the South counted as two-thirds of a person when determining the population entitled to congressional representation. As a result, New England was falling into minority status in the Congress. This measure was designed to prevent that.

*A political cartoon of the Hartford Convention of 1814. The inclinations toward secession by Rhode Island, Massachusetts, and Connecticut are satirized, with encouragement from Britain's king, George III.*

The Treaty of Ghent ended the war in late 1814. (One last battle would be fought early in 1815.) This pretty much cut the rug out from under the Hartford Convention. It had no way of enforcing the decisions it had reached. When word leaked out about its discussion of secession, public response was strongly negative. With the war over, even rank-and-file New Englanders felt the convention had gone too far.

Prior to the War of 1812, antiwar sentiments had sprung mostly from religious conviction. During it, economic considerations fueled the New England antiwar movement. In the U.S. wars that would follow, humanist principles of antiviolence and passive resistance would emerge and causes would clash. Peace organizations would form and fail and rise again. The argument would be made that war is an innate part of humanity. Always there would be people to stand up, for whatever reason, to declare that the same is true of peace.

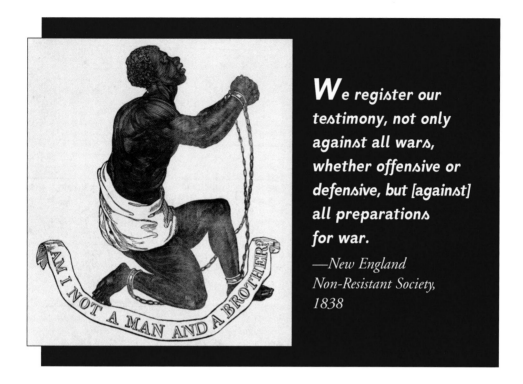

> **W**e register our testimony, not only against all wars, whether offensive or defensive, but [against] all preparations for war.
>
> —*New England Non-Resistant Society, 1838*

# Mr. Polk's War

**R**evulsion against the bloodletting of the War of 1812 inspired Unitarian minister William Ellery Channing, known as "the apostle of Unitarianism," and Congregationalist reverend Noah Worcester to organize the Massachusetts Peace Society. Reverend Worcester's devotion of time and energy to this cause was so wholehearted that he often deprived himself of basic necessities such as food and clothing to promote the society and peace. At this time—1815 and the years that followed—David Low Dodge, a well-off New York merchant, was inserting peace pamphlets into the packages of the goods he sold. William Ladd, a sea captain who became a Maine farmer, poured funds into the Massachusetts Peace Society treasury and devoted his life to promoting its principles. Long after he became an invalid with ulcerated legs, he continued to write and lecture for the cause. In 1828 Ladd founded the American Peace Society (APS).

The APS was a flawed effort to link together under one organizational umbrella the many small local peace societies that had come into being in the early 1800s. William Lloyd Garrison was attracted to the organization. Garrison was the Boston-based publisher of the *Liberator,* an influential antislavery journal. A leader of the abolitionist cause to free slaves everywhere in the United States, Garrison was a man of strong—many thought stubborn—principles. He spoke out for women's equality, and his antiwar views were particularly uncompromising. He believed in the "immediate end of conflict with no compromises or gradual measures in between." The APS leaned more

*In 1828 William Ladd* (left) *founded the American Peace Society, an association that tried to organize many smaller local peace societies. His efforts met with limited success, despite the strong support of abolitionist William Lloyd Garrison* (right).

toward a step-by-step approach, dealing with conflict situations or threats of war one at a time.

## THE ROAD TO WAR

In September 1838, an APS convention was held in Boston. Roughly two hundred people attended the three-day conference. One group of male APS delegates, however, remained only a few hours. They stormed out in protest because the APS was accepting women as full members. Those who remained organized themselves into a new group of men and women, the New England Non-Resistant Society. They adopted the following statement of principles written by Garrison:

> We register our testimony, not only against all wars, whether offensive or defensive, but all preparations for war; against every naval ship, every arsenal, every fortification; against the militia system and a standing army; against all military chieftains and soldiers; against all monuments commemorative of victory over a foreign foe, all trophies won in battle, all celebration in honor of military or naval exploits; against all appropriations for the defense of a nation by force and arms, on the part of any legislative body; against every edict of government requiring of its subjects military service. Hence, we deem it unlawful to bear arms or to hold military office.

At this time, two issues drew the focus of peace organizations. The first was the so-called Oregon Question. This involved the Pacific Northwest, an area lying below latitude 54 degrees, 40 minutes and, by treaty, controlled jointly by the United States and by Britain's colony, Canada. A growing U.S. movement, led by congressional Democrats, wanted to take over the area by force. "Fifty-four forty or fight!" was the war cry, and peace activists were kept busy with letters and petitions aimed at staving off yet another war with Britain.

*A political cartoon from 1846 belittles the self-interested attitudes of Europe toward the dispute on how to settle the northern boundary of American territory in Oregon.*

They were kept even busier trying to avert war with Mexico over Texas and California. In a revolution against Spain, which had colonized it, Mexico had won its independence in 1821. At that time, Texas, California, New Mexico, Utah, Nevada, Arizona, and a portion of Colorado were all part of Mexico. In 1836 Texas had separated from Mexico and had declared itself the Lone Star Republic. American settlers had been moving westward to California, and the cry of Manifest Destiny was once more being sounded throughout the land. The United States would stretch from sea to shining sea. Annexing Texas was a key part of this vision. In 1845, when Congress accepted Texas into the Union as a state, the Mexican government broke off diplomatic relations with the United States.

## "STIPULATED ARBITRATION"

The United States claimed that the southern boundary of Texas was the Rio Grande. However, before Texas joined the Union, no Texans had settled south of the Nueces River. President James K. Polk wanted Mexico to agree to the Rio Grande boundary and to sell California to the United States. The Mexicans would not agree to either proposition. Polk ordered U.S. troops to occupy the territory between the two rivers. They clashed with Mexican patrols, and American blood was shed. War followed. Antiwar critics labeled it "Mr. Polk's War," and the designation stuck.

Before and during the war, both the APS and the New England Non-Resistant Society actively opposed it. Following William Ladd's death, his followers had concentrated on a project of "stipulated arbitration," which called for a "Court of Nations composed of the most able jurists in the world" to settle disputes between countries. They successfully campaigned for the Massachusetts Senate to adopt resolutions approving arbitration, rather than war, as the means of settling international disputes. A similar resolution worked its way through the U.S. Congress before, during, and after the Mexican-American War (1846–1848) but was eventually tabled.

At this time, renowned journalist and feminist Margaret Fuller, an avowed pacifist, was covering a revolution by peasants against their feudal masters in Italy. The experience had given her doubts that violence could be avoided in "fighting giant wrongs." If the rights of the people could not be obtained any other way, she wrote, "I am not sure that I can keep my hands free from blood."

## WILL SLAVERY SPREAD?

For most Americans, the conflict with Mexico was not simply a matter of war or peace. There were underlying issues that shaped attitudes toward the Mexican War. In an article approving the annexation of Texas, the *Washington Union* predicted that "the road to California will

be open to us." It went on to forecast that "a corps of properly organized volunteers . . . would invade, overrun, and occupy Mexico. They
would enable us not only to take California, but to keep it."

Some northerners were in favor of acquiring California because
they saw it as an opportunity for expanding markets through seaports
on the Pacific. They were not, however, in favor of going to war to
seize California. Many of them were afraid that this might result in
creating another slave state. Annexation of Texas had already tipped
the balance, so that, in 1847, the Union had fifteen slave states to
fourteen free states. The industrial North feared that the agrarian,
slaveholding South would control the country. James Russell Lowell
summed up this fear in a poem:

> They just want this Californy
> So's to lug new slave states in
> To abuse ye, an' to scorn ye,
> An' to plunder ye like sin.

This issue was also of major concern to antiwar crusaders. Pacifist
Lydia Maria Child had published the first U.S. antislavery book, *An
Appeal in Favor of That Class of Americans Called Africans.* She
insisted that "abolition principles and nonresistance seem to me iden-
tical." Almost all members of the two major antiwar organizations
were against slavery. Female members were also concerned with wom-
en's suffrage and other women's issues.

## YOUNG MR. LINCOLN

Mr. Polk's War, like other wars, had its prominent antiwar spokespersons who were regarded—if only briefly—as heroes. To take a public
stand against war in the face of nationwide patriotic fervor requires
courage. Subsequent war-making actions don't detract from such a
stand, but they may blot out the memory of it.

In 1846 Abraham Lincoln was elected to Congress from Illinois as a Whig. The Whigs were a major U.S. political party from 1834 to 1854 and were eventually replaced by the Republican Party. Lincoln was a member of a Whig minority faction that opposed the war. As a freshman member of Congress, he rose to challenge President Polk to specify the exact spot where American blood was shed "on the American soil." The speech came close to calling the president a liar in having made such a claim when demanding a declaration of war from Congress.

Lincoln persisted in confronting Polk as the war continued. Speaking in the House of Representatives on July 27, 1848, he repeated charges that "the war was unnecessarily and unconstitutionally commenced by the President." Addressing Polk specifically, he added that "marching an army into the midst of a peaceful Mexican settlement, frightening the inhabitants away, leaving their growing crops and other property to destruction, to you may appear a perfectly amiable, peaceful, unprovoking procedure; but it does not appear so to us."

## GO DIRECTLY TO JAIL!

Henry David Thoreau was not a politician like Lincoln, but his protest against the Mexican War created a legend and a standard for antiwar opposition that has persisted to the present day. He was not a member of any pacifist or antiwar organization. He also refused to join abolitionist groups or political parties. A philosopher and a poet, he believed that the individual must think through issues for himself or herself to decide what is right. Then the person must act on that decision.

As the war with Mexico was beginning, Thoreau had come to believe it was being waged on behalf of slaveholders bent on extending their slave territory. He had long been convinced that slavery was evil and had written that, "I cannot for an instant recognize that political organization as my government which is the slave's government also." Because of his opposition to slavery, since 1842, Thoreau had

*Thoreau's technique of protesting war by noncooperation with the government, even if it results in jail time, has served as a model for subsequent protest movements.*

refused to pay the Massachusetts poll tax. This was a tax levied on each citizen to support the state government. When the Mexican War started, Thoreau regarded the poll tax as money used to promote the conflict.

In July 1846, Thoreau was arrested and jailed for not paying the tax. The story goes that while Thoreau was in jail, his friend the Transcendentalist philosopher Ralph Waldo Emerson visited him. "Henry, why are you here?" Emerson is said to have asked. "Waldo," replied Thoreau, "why are you *not* here?"

The answer went to the core of Thoreau's belief. "Under a government which imprisons any unjustly," he wrote, "the true place for a just man is also a prison."

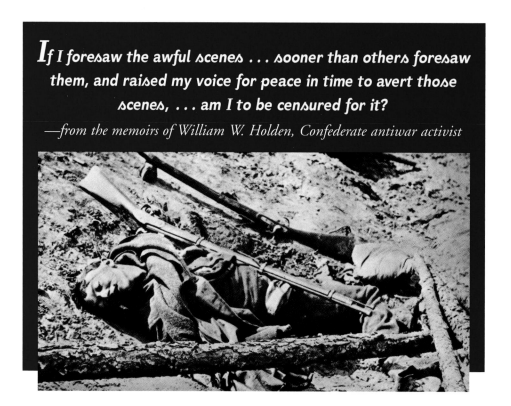

> *If I foresaw the awful scenes . . . sooner than others foresaw them, and raised my voice for peace in time to avert those scenes, . . . am I to be censured for it?*
>
> —*from the memoirs of William W. Holden, Confederate antiwar activist*

# NORTH VERSUS SOUTH

Conflicting loyalties split the peace movement before and during the Civil War (1861–1865). Prominent pacifists justified violence in the cause of abolishing slavery. Among them were Massachusetts senator Charles Sumner; George C. Beckwith, who had become the dominant figure in the APS after the death of William Ladd; and Henry David Thoreau.

Before the war, Thoreau had heard John Brown speak in Concord, Massachusetts. Brown was raising money to arm a force to free slaves in the South. Thoreau was moved to make a small contribution to

*At Harpers Ferry, Virginia, U.S. Marines, under the command of Colonel Robert E. Lee, smash the armory door behind which John Brown and his men are trapped in 1859.*

Brown's cause. On October 16, 1859, Brown led a raid on the federal armory at Harpers Ferry, a strip of rocky land located where the two rivers marking the boundary between western Virginia and Maryland meet. Ten men, including two of John Brown's sons, died in the raid. Brown himself was caught and hanged.

One of Brown's men had escaped and had fled to Massachusetts, where Thoreau helped him flee to Canada. Thoreau wrote a tribute, *The Last Days of John Brown,* in which he characterized Brown's life "as a principled struggle against the evils of slavery." He wrote of Brown that "he has earned immortality."

## THE INEVITABLE CONFLICT

John Brown was the most violent of the abolitionists. That an icon of nonviolence like Thoreau should have glorified him was an indication of how torn pacifists were between principles of nonviolence and the goal of ending slavery. At the same time, writes Professor Merle Curti, in the days leading up to the Civil War, "the organized friends of peace for once found themselves with the majority. The bulk of the American people preferred some sort of compromise and conciliation to bloodshed. Even in the South . . . there was no overwhelming desire for conflict."

In the chaotic weeks before war broke out, mass meetings took place throughout the North and some in the South, each calling for avoiding war. Peace petitions signed by hundreds of thousands of people poured into Congress—truly an impressive response for those pre-Internet days. Merchants and bankers of the North and South warned of the impact on trade and the economy. Debt collection for cotton previously sold to the North and machinery sold to the South would not be possible. Labor leaders warned that workers would bear the brunt of the war, do most of the fighting, and suffer most from the economic impact.

South Carolina seceded from the Union on December 20, 1860. By February 1861, six other Southern states had followed. That month, a peace conference was held in Washington, D.C. This was not a conference in which pacifist groups or their members participated. Rather, it was a gathering of prominent civic leaders making a last-ditch effort to head off civil war. The words spoken by many of them sounded as if they came from an antiwar pamphlet, but they were uttered in vain. Peace was not to be.

On May 27, 1861, with the war under way, the APS met at the Park Street Church in Boston. The attitude of most—but not all—of those present was to justify the war rather than to end it. "The catastrophe that had come was not a war" in their eyes; "it was rather a gigantic rebellion to be suppressed by the police power of the government." Gerrit Smith, vice president of the society, did not attend the meeting. At an earlier date, facing the prospect of slavery spreading into Kansas, he had declared that, "I and ten thousand other peace men are not only ready to have it repulsed with violence, but pursued even unto death with violence." But in 1861, he sent the convention a message calling "slavery . . . the source of war" and concluded that doing away with slavery would be a giant step toward doing away with war altogether.

## PERSECUTING COPPERHEADS

The women of the New England Non-Resistant Society were fragmented by lack of leadership and different commitments during the Civil War. Their leader for pacifism had been William Lloyd Garrison. He had become a vocal supporter of Abraham Lincoln and an advocate of pursuing the war until emancipation was obtained. Some peace women also justified the war on the basis of granting slaves their freedom. Others, committed to woman suffrage (the demand that women be granted the right to vote), feared that the stress being put on obtaining rights for slaves was at the expense of the battle for the rights of women. Still others clung to their pacifist beliefs and pursued them by risking their lives behind the front lines to nurse wounded soldiers. In the South, peace women stood by their principles in the face of fierce opposition.

In the North, members of the Democratic Party who were Union loyalists were known as "copperheads," after a common snake. They were for restoring the Union but against destroying the old South to do it. Republicans regarded their attitude as opposition to the war itself. By 1862 many copperheads were being labeled supporters of the rebellion and subjected to military arrest. Copperhead sentiment flourished in border states like Kentucky and Tennessee. There, and in northeastern states as well, the government jailed copperheads for opposing emancipation as a government war aim.

The copperheads were more formally known as Peace Democrats. In 1863 former congressman Clement L. Vallandigham emerged as their leader. Running for governor of Ohio, he condemned the "wicked, cruel and unnecessary war" being fought "for the purpose of crushing out liberty and creating a despotism . . . a war for the freedom of the blacks and the enslavement of the whites."

*Peace Party candidate C. L. Vallandigham is arrested in 1863 after stating his pacifist views in a campaign speech.*

Following this speech, General Ambrose E. Burnside had Vallandigham arrested for treason. Even as he was being tried by a military court and convicted of expressing "disloyal sentiments and opinions," Vallandigham's followers were setting afire the offices of Ohio's leading Republican newspaper in protest. President Lincoln set aside the prison sentence Vallandigham received and ordered him exiled instead. He was escorted under a flag of truce to Southern lines and turned over to the Confederates. Subsequently Vallandigham made his way to Canada, where he continued to wage his campaign for governor of Ohio as a Peace Party candidate. He was not, however, elected.

# FIGHT OR PAY

Outside of the Confederacy itself, New York City had more antiwar opposition than any other place in the Civil War North. At the start of the war, the U.S. census showed the city, which consisted only of Manhattan Island, to have a population of 813,669. Half of the population was foreign born. The overwhelming majority of foreign born were Irish.

The large Irish migration to the United States had begun in the 1840s as a result of the potato famine in Ireland. The famine had impoverished the country, and the influx of Irish to the United States was still continuing when the Civil War started. These new immigrants were very poor. With jobs scarce, many of them were recruited into the army both before and during the war. In the beginning years of the conflict, it was a common practice for U.S. recruiting officers to meet ships from Ireland and recruit new immigrants right off the dock.

Some of the Irish who were already here objected to that practice, but many did not. They regarded the new arrivals as potential rivals for jobs and were just as glad to see them siphoned off into the army. Then, in March 1863, Congress passed the Conscription Act, strongly opposed by a New York Irish political organization called the Knights of the Golden Circle. The law was enforced as a lottery in which men were assigned numbers. The numbers were drawn from a small spinning cage to determine who must serve in the military. The fury of opposition to the draft law focused on a clause that allowed any drafted man to avoid service by paying the government three hundred dollars. It was a rare New York City Irishman in the 1860s who could earn that much money in the course of a year. Feeding the fury were persistent rumors that the underlying reason of the war was to provide wealthy Northern manufacturers with freed black slaves who could be hired at low wages. These African American workers would dispossess Irish workers and bust the few unions that the Irish had managed to organize.

## IRISH ON THE MARCH

On Saturday, July 11, 1863, the first 1,236 names of men to be drafted were drawn. Among them was the fireman leader of Volunteer Engine Company No. Thirty-Three, which was nicknamed the Black Joke and was infamous for its brawls with other gangs in Manhattan. Learning that the rest of the numbers were to be drawn the following Monday, the Black Joke made plans to destroy the conscription office and its records.

When the draft office opened that Monday, someone fired a pistol and the men of the Black Joke stampeded the office. Behind them was a howling mob carrying placards proclaiming "No Draft!" and banners proclaiming "Down with the Protestants!" The Black Joke torched the draft office. When another fire company arrived and tried to put out the flames, the mob attacked them, forcing them to flee for their lives.

Meanwhile, several armed mobs of both men and women marched out of the mostly Irish slums of lower Manhattan and began assembling in a vacant lot east of Central Park. The gathering numbered between five thousand and fifteen thousand people. Armed with clubs and pitchforks, knives and some guns, the mob headed for the state armory where they hoped to acquire more weapons. En route to the armory, the Invalid Corps, a unit made up of disabled soldiers, met them. When the mob charged the soldiers, the Invalid Corps fired their rifles, wounding six men and one woman.

Despite this setback, the mob succeeded in reaching the armory, which was plundered of carbines and ammunition. As they left, they were ambushed by a contingent of police who killed several rioters with their clubs before retreating. The mob then set fire to the armory. It was an old wooden building, and the resulting fire was spectacular and quickly spread to nearby structures. While it was burning, a second mob was surging "across Manhattan Island from the Hudson to the East rivers, looting, burning, and beating every Negro who dared show himself. Three black men were hanged before

*The draft riots broke out as a result of the Conscription Act, which was discriminatory to immigrants. Between July 11 and 16, 1863, about two thousand New Yorkers were killed and an additional eight thousand were injured.*

nightfall on the first day of the rioting, and thereafter an average of three a day were found by the police hanging to trees and lamp-posts, their bodies slashed by knives or beaten almost to a pulp."

Toward nightfall, this mob gathered in front of the Colored Orphan Asylum on Fifth Avenue and Forty-third Street. The four-story brick structure housed two hundred African American children under twelve years of age. When the mob stormed the building, the superintendent of the asylum, William E. Davis, barricaded the front doors and marched the children out the back way. However, one little girl was left behind. After crashing through the barricades, the mob pilfered the bedding, clothing, and toys the children had abandoned. When they found the little girl hiding under a bed, they killed her.

The riots went on for six days. Many wealthy homes on upper Fifth Avenue were vandalized and looted. Many businesses from newsstands to high-priced jewelry stores were broken into and robbed. Eventually troops came in, preceded by ships with artillery that fired on the rioters. It is estimated that two thousand people were killed in the New York City draft riots and eight thousand wounded. Every man on the force suffered injuries, and three policemen died. Eighteen African Americans were hanged. Five drowned when mobs chased them into the East and Hudson rivers, and seventy others simply disappeared, many of them presumed killed. Property loss was estimated at about five million dollars. It was the most violent such protest in American history.

## THE SOUTH'S ANTIWAR PROTESTS

Antiwar protest was less violent in the South during the Civil War, but various peace organizations had appeared there by 1863. The Confederate army had introduced conscription early in the war, and some—mostly poor—men had taken steps to avoid it. As the war began to go badly, desertions became a cause of concern in the Confederate army. Increasing numbers "of these deserters joined with draft evaders in back country regions to form guerilla bands that resisted Confederate authority and virtually ruled whole counties."

Some of these groups formed ties with secret antiwar societies or formed new peace groups. Among these organizations was the Peace and Constitutional Society in Arkansas, the Peace Society in northern Alabama and northern Georgia, and the Order of Heroes of America in western North Carolina and eastern Tennessee. In North Carolina, the Heroes of America peace movement had a powerful ally in William W. Holden, publisher of the *North Carolina Standard.*

*In 1865, immediately after the Civil War, President Andrew Johnson appointed William Holden (left) governor of North Carolina.*

Holden attacked Confederate administration policies throughout the war and protested the draft as military despotism. Working with the Heroes of America, Holden and his collaborators organized more than a hundred antiwar meetings calling for negotiations for an honorable peace. According to one critic, at these meetings "the most treasonable language was uttered, and Union flags raised." Finally, a Confederate brigade commanded by General James Longstreet wrecked and plundered the *North Carolina Standard* offices. The next day, Holden's reporters demolished a rival, prowar Confederate newspaper.

On February 24, 1864, Holden was forced to stop publication of the *Standard*. This, however, did not stop the Southern peace movement. Holden's insistence that the Civil War was a "rich man's war/poor man's fight" was widely affirmed by rank-and-file soldiers in the South and the North.

*T*he forcible annexation of the Philippine Islands is not necessary to make the United States a world power.

—*William Jennings Bryan, 1899*

# ISLANDS IN THE SUN

About 620,000 soldiers lost their lives during the four years of the Civil War. As historian James McPherson points out, "The Civil War's cost in American lives was as great as in all of the nation's other wars combined through Vietnam." During the decades that followed, peace—as an alternative to war—was more popular with the American people than at any time during the hundred-odd years of the nation's history. Despite this, the dissension over abolition and women's rights that had shattered the unity of peace organizations during the war persisted in its aftermath.

During the post–Civil War period, women's peace organizations such as the New England Non-Resistant Society tended to be based locally and to emphasize different goals. Some stressed suffrage. Others focused on improving social conditions. Some groups allied themselves with the international peace movement starting up in Europe. A few sent representatives to the 1892 founding conference of the International Peace Bureau held in Bern, Switzerland. The membership of the APS had dropped to only four hundred people by 1892.

## THE UNIVERSAL PEACE UNION

At the same time, however, a new and dynamic group had emerged to campaign for the cause of peace. This was the Universal Peace Union (UPU), founded by former members of the APS who had been turned off by the dissension in that organization. The UPU was formed in 1866 in Providence, Rhode Island. It called for "immediate disarmament" of all nations and "an agreement to submit to arbitration" any differences between nations. Alfred Love was elected president of the UPU and served in that position until his death in 1913.

*The aptly named Alfred Love was the founder and president of the Universal Peace Union, an organization that called for immediate disarmament of all nations.*

Love has been described as a "modest, shy whimsical man" who "in spite of stubbornness and eccentricities" was "a leader capable of inspiring loyalty and affection." His personality dominated the UPU, and his instinct for the importance of symbolism and music influenced peace movements for the next hundred years and more. He conducted ceremonies in which military swords were actually beaten into plowshares. Hymns of peace and other antiwar songs rang out over the picnic grounds when UPU meetings were held. He felt that such demonstrations and music might move ordinary people toward peace more powerfully than speeches could.

In the end, however, it was words that weakened the cause of Love and the UPU. In 1896, in an effort to head off the Spanish-American War (1898), the UPU begged the Spanish government to withdraw from its Cuban colony. Love sent a letter to the queen of Spain that began, "We want you to hear from the real representatives of the American heart." The letter was intercepted and published in newspapers in a garbled form that made it appear treasonous. The public was outraged. The UPU Philadelphia headquarters were trashed. Alfred Love was burned in effigy, the charred dummy used for target practice and slashed apart by swords.

## "THE SPLENDID LITTLE ISLAND"

In a sense, Love was a victim of the changes sweeping over the nation in the 1890s. By then the United States had built up agriculturally and industrially. Businesspeople had a growing ambition to develop new markets and investment opportunities beyond the nation's borders. Additional markets would create jobs for U.S. workers. Some labor unions and working people looked favorably on such expansion.

It was natural that expansionists, as they were called, should contemplate Spanish-ruled Cuba, only ninety miles off the coast of Florida. Senator Henry Cabot Lodge of Massachusetts called Cuba "the splendid little island, one of the richest spots on the face of the earth." He added that "free Cuba would mean a great market for the United States [and] an opportunity for American capital." Actually, U.S. trade with Cuba already averaged $100 million a year, and U.S. bankers and businesspeople had $50 million invested in Cuba. If Cuba were no longer under Spanish rule, it would be open to much more profitable development by the United States.

Expansionists were blessed with a noble principle for coveting Cuba. In 1895 a rebellion against the Spanish who colonized the island had erupted. Spain had ruled Cuba since 1511, nineteen years after Columbus first landed there. The regime had been cruel and oppressive. Sugar was the chief product of the island, and Spain had seized all of the farms and plantations on which sugarcane was grown. Wealthy Spaniards controlled the economy, and the native Cubans, along with the descendants of the African slaves the Spaniards had imported, lived in poverty.

Sympathy for the Cuban rebels was widespread in the United States. This sentiment was raised to a fever pitch by the newspapers of William Randolph Hearst and Joseph Pulitzer. The prospect of war boosted circulation tremendously. Pulitzer's *New York World* sold a record five million copies in one week. In a famous interchange, Hearst artist Frederic Remington wired Hearst from Cuba that, "THERE WILL BE NO WAR," and Hearst replied, "YOU FURNISH PICTURES. I WILL FURNISH WAR."

## "REMEMBER THE *MAINE!*"

By this time, the APS was re-establishing its role as a prominent organization in the antiwar movement under the leadership of Benjamin Franklin Trueblood. A Quaker, Trueblood was one of the few full-time salaried leaders in the peace movement. He headed the APS from 1892 to 1915 and was responsible for increasing its membership from four hundred to eight thousand.

*Benjamin Trueblood in his office at the American Peace Society, an organization he headed from 1892 to 1915.*

Dr. Trueblood was instrumental in promoting peace petitions and lobbying efforts to persuade President William McKinley to withstand the pressure to go to war with Spain. Together with other peace groups, the APS established a lobby of eight or nine pacifist workers to persuade senators and representatives to resist the campaign for war. Under Dr. Trueblood, the APS had adopted a policy of working to prevent wars from occurring in the belief that, once they started, it was futile to try to stop them. Their most concerted effort followed the explosion that sank the U.S. battleship *Maine* in Havana Harbor on February 15, 1898.

The Spanish government claimed it was an accident. "A prompt inquiry" by the U.S. Navy "failed to blame Spain." Nevertheless, the

Hearst *New York Journal* reported that the two hundred sixty U.S. sailors who died had been the victims of "an enemy's secret infernal machine." The cry of "REMEMBER THE MAINE!" was raised throughout the land. Both the APS and the UPU fought a last-ditch campaign to avert war. Telegrams and letters urging arbitration and a peaceful solution deluged Congress and the president. Assistant Secretary of the Navy Theodore Roosevelt was "amazed and horrified at the peace-at-any-price telegrams from New York, Boston, and elsewhere to the president and senators."

The war with Spain over Cuba was short. It began on April 25, 1898, and ended on August 12 when U.S. military superiority forced the Spanish to sue for peace.

## OPERATION PHILIPPINES

Meanwhile, the U.S. military also sought conquest of the Philippines, another of Spain's longtime colonies. Ten days after the *Maine* went down, Secretary of the Navy John D. Long went to visit his osteopath, leaving Assistant Secretary Roosevelt in charge of his office. Roosevelt immediately cabled Commodore George Dewey in Hong Kong to assemble his ships. In case of war, Roosevelt wanted Dewey to begin "OFFENSIVE OPERATIONS IN THE PHILIPPINE ISLANDS."

Admiral Dewey destroyed the Spanish fleet in the Philippines, and on August 13, the Spanish surrendered the Philippine capital city of Manila. The remnants of a Filipino revolutionary movement, led by Emilio Aguinaldo, welcomed U.S. forces as liberators. On December 10, 1898, the United States and Spain signed the Treaty of Paris, in which Spain granted Cuba independence, turned over Puerto Rico to the United States, and sold the Philippines to the United States for twenty million dollars.

Senator Lodge insisted that "we must on no account let the islands go. . . . We hold the other side of the Pacific, and the value to this country is almost beyond imagination." President McKinley asserted that "the insurgents and all others must recognize the military occupation and authority of the United States."

But Admiral Dewey had assured Aguinaldo that the United States was "rich in territory and money, and needed no colonies." Aguinaldo believed he had Dewey's word of honor that the Philippines would be granted their freedom once the Spanish had been vanquished. However, as additional American troops landed and U.S. military rule was extended over more and more territory, Aguinaldo concluded that he had been betrayed and prepared for war. Hostilities began in January 1899.

In response to the Philippine occupation, the Anti-Imperialist League (A-IL) was organized. Its founders included some of the most prominent business leaders, intellectuals, and politicians in the country. The A-IL specifically opposed "the new American policy of imperialism which sought to obtain part of the overseas empires being divided up by Europe and Japan." Its membership would eventually grow to over thirty thousand, making it "the largest anti-war organization . . . in American history" up to that time.

## THE ANTI-IMPERIALIST LEAGUE

George Boutwell, a former governor of Massachusetts, was elected president of the A-IL. Former president Grover Cleveland, industrialist Andrew Carnegie, and philosopher William James were among its founding members. The highest principles motivated these men, but some of them were afflicted by racist fears as well. A-IL member and former Missouri senator Carl Schurz was fearful that annexing the Philippines would bring an influx of "more or less barbarous Asiatics" into the United States. William James's concerns were more humane. Responding to reports of atrocities committed by U.S. soldiers against Filipino civilians, he thundered "God damn the U.S. for its vile conduct in the Philippine Isles."

The A-IL dispensed more than one million leaflets, pamphlets, and brochures opposing the seizure of the Philippines. Its most prominent spokesperson was William Jennings Bryan, who had also been a founding member. Bryan had run for president in 1896 and had been defeated by William McKinley. In 1899 Bryan had insisted that "the forcible annexation of the Philippine Islands is not necessary to make the United States a world power." In 1900 he was preparing to

*One of the many leaflets dispersed by the Anti-Imperialist League protesting the seizure of the Philippines*

*William Jennings Bryan was a Democratic presidential candidate who ran on an anti-imperialist platform at the turn of the twentieth century.*

run against McKinley again, and his opposition to the Philippine conquest was a key part of his campaign.

Bryan successfully urged that an anti-imperialism statement be inserted in the 1900 Democratic Party platform. When he was nominated, he devoted his acceptance speech to criticism of the war in the Philippines, which by that time was becoming increasingly bloody. His position was bolstered by letters from soldiers in the Philippines that accused the administration of underreporting U.S. casualties and by verified accounts of atrocities being committed by American forces in response to similar outrages by Aguinaldo's forces.

A Republican political machine—backed by business interests eager to exploit the Philippines and to maintain the incumbent McKinley in office—proved too powerful for Bryan to overcome. McKinley was reelected, with Theodore Roosevelt as his vice president. A few months after his inauguration in 1901, McKinley was assassinated. Theodore Roosevelt became president. A champion of expansionism in the Pacific, President Roosevelt enthusiastically backed U.S. forces in the Philippines through 1902, when Aguinaldo and the rebels were decisively defeated.

After Bryan's loss, the government had threatened to prosecute antiwar activists for treason, and support for the A-IL fell away. Its membership shrank, and with the end of the war, it was widely regarded as irrelevant. According to some historians, however, the campaign of the A-IL did have one lasting effect. In their view, the expansionist political forces in the United States turned away from outright conquest and colonialism to more indirect and benevolent forms of domination over underdeveloped countries. As for American peace activism, the war clouds that were already gathering over Europe would reinvigorate it in ways that would influence antiwar movements through the beginning of the next century.

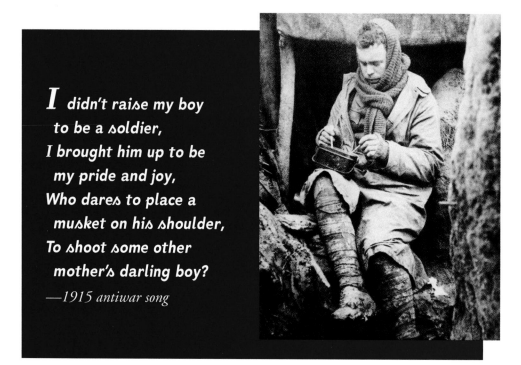

*I* didn't raise my boy
to be a soldier,
I brought him up to be
my pride and joy,
Who dares to place a
musket on his shoulder,
To shoot some other
mother's darling boy?
—*1915 antiwar song*

# THE WAR TO END
# ALL WARS

**A**fter the Philippines were successfully occupied by American troops, the peace movement in the United States was fragmented but growing. Established organizations like the UPU and the APS were regrouping. New peace groups were forming across the country. In 1904, when the Boston Peace Congress convened, the three thousand people in attendance represented almost two hundred organizations. These included churches and synagogues, women's clubs, merchants' associations, and trade unions.

Secretary of State John Hay addressed the group, as did philosopher William James and UPU president Alfred Love. A resolution was introduced by Love committing the Boston Peace Congress to the abolition of armaments. He also made a motion to condemn private and public loans to wartime belligerents and the sale of any supplies used for waging war. Both motions were defeated. The influx of new groups, particularly business groups, had introduced a new conservatism to the peace movement. New converts were interpreting peace in different ways.

## FIRST NATIONAL PEACE CONGRESS

Two years after the Boston Peace Congress, the New York Peace Society (NYPS) was organized with wealthy industrialist Andrew Carnegie as president. Its original membership included prominent New York City business leaders, philanthropists, journalists, lawyers, and clergy. These people had great influence, and they enlisted people from the topmost ranks of society in their cause. Carnegie was lavish in spending his money to build up the organization.

In 1907 Carnegie and the NYPS organized the first National Peace Congress. It was attended by ten mayors, nineteen members of Congress, four Supreme Court justices, two presidential candidates, thirty labor leaders, forty bishops, sixty newspaper editors, and twenty-seven millionaires. What it lacked was any significant support from the lower—or even the middle—classes. Nevertheless, it gave the American peace movement great prestige among foreign leaders.

That same year, the second Hague Peace Conference was held in the Netherlands. The first one had met there in 1899—after a proposal by Czar Nicholas II of Russia for all nations to join in a congress for the limitation of armaments had startled the world. His was the most repressive regime in Europe, and Russian armies had routinely extended the Russian Empire by swallowing up whole nations. Why would he propose a meeting for peace?

## QUESTIONS OF MOTIVES

Twenty-six nations including the United States had attended the 1899 Hague Peace Conference. Leading anti-imperialist Edwin Lawrence Godkin, editor of both the *Nation* and the *New York Evening Post,* noted that it was being held at a time when the United States had committed itself to "the military spirit and idea of forcible conquest." American expansionists suspected that the Hague conference was bent on restricting U.S. imperialism and competition for world markets.

Suspicion of the czar's motives was widespread among conference participants, and it was justified. The idea for a peace conference came from the czar's ministers who recognized that Russian armaments development was lagging dangerously behind that of Germany, France, and Austria. The czar and his advisers regarded peace as a necessary policy while Russia played catch-up.

The 1899 Hague Peace Conference failed to achieve its objective of limiting armaments. The 1907 conference also failed to reach any arms limitation agreements. In addition, it did not renew the declaration of the previous convention limiting poison gas and so-called dumdum bullets, which are designed to do maximum damage after penetrating a target's flesh.

## SHALL WORKERS FIGHT WORKERS?

Also in 1907, the Socialist International, made up of the Socialist parties of Europe, held a congress in Stuttgart, Germany. Vladimir Lenin, the Russian Bolshevik leader and future first head of the Union of Soviet Socialist Republics, introduced a resolution that the congress adopted. It pledged the working classes of all nations and their representatives to work to prevent the outbreak of war. However, if war broke out, while working to end it, they were to "exploit the crisis with all their strength to hasten the abolition of capitalism."

Lenin had been influenced by Karl Marx's *Communist Manifesto*. Working people, it had declared, "have no country" and would not

*The antiwar movement went well beyond American borders. This French peace advocate is demonstrating outside the 1907 international Hague Peace Conference in the Netherlands.*

fight against each other in a war. Not all Socialists, however, agreed with Marx and Lenin.

Many of those attending the congress proclaimed their patriotism as a higher duty than the betterment of the working class. Typical was a statement by a member of the German delegation. "It is not true that workers have no Fatherland," he insisted. "The love of humanity does not prevent us from being good Germans."

In America, Socialist Party leader Eugene V. Debs had been an early and outspoken opponent of American military action in the Philippines. He had spoken against it as a working man and as a champion of the working class. He presented his antiwar position with frankly Socialist rhetoric, proclaiming that "war is national murder, that the poor furnish the victims and that whatever the outcome may be, the effect is always the same upon the toiling class."

*Eugene V. Debs, a Socialist Party presidential candidate, campaigns in a railroad yard.*

## EUGENE V. DEBS

Debs had been one of a small group of people who organized the Socialist Party in the United States. He would be the party's five-time presidential candidate and leader until his death in 1926. Prior to becoming a Socialist, Debs had been a charismatic leader of the American labor movement. At the age of fourteen, he had gone to work in the railroad yards, working his way up to become a loco-motive fireman. After organizing a local lodge of the Brotherhood of Locomotive Firemen, he was elected national treasurer and secretary of the parent organization. He later became president of the Ameri-can Railway Union and subsequently led a successful strike against the Great Northern Railroad for higher wages. He also led a workers' walkout against the Chicago Pullman Palace Car Company. When he defied a federal injunction prohibiting the action, he had been sentenced to six months in jail. He was converted to Socialism after reading Karl Marx and other radical thinkers in prison.

In 1908 Debs presided over a giant meeting of the U.S. Socialist Party held in the New York Hippodrome. He argued that the end of war would come only with the end of competition. He called for a general strike of U.S. workers together with workers of other nations to stop the machinery of war should that prove necessary. Rank-and-file Socialists approved this program. At the same time, many of them supported the less radical programs of the conventional antiwar organizations.

Even pro-peace Americans were leery of Socialist antiwar programs. There was a feeling that Socialism itself was a foreign doctrine and possibly un-American. It had, after all, sprung from the theories of Karl Marx, theories that had also spawned Bolshevism, Communism, and anarchism. Although Socialists like Debs rejected much of the philosophies of these groups and were not affiliated with them, Americans often did not distinguish among them. In the public mind, Socialists were considered extremists and were confused with violent, bomb-throwing anarchists. Anarchists, after all, had assassinated President Carnot of France, Premier Canovas of Spain, Empress Elizabeth of Austria, King Humbert of Italy, and President McKinley of the United States. Although Socialists were nonviolent, the distinction was blurred in the public mind.

At the same time, Socialist ideas were taking root in the United States, incited by the hardships spawned by the Industrial Revolution. The exploitation of labor—low pay, poor working conditions, and safety hazards—had given birth to such organizations as the International Workers of the World, the American Federation of Labor, the International Ladies Garment Workers Union, the American Railway Union, and others. These were not Socialist organizations, but their demands echoed many of the pro-labor principles of the Socialist Party. When push came to shove for these unions, however, patriotism would usually prevail over solidarity with the workers of other countries.

## THE WOMAN'S PEACE PARTY

Socialist antiwar principles were a far cry from those of Andrew Carnegie. In December 1910, he launched the Carnegie Endowment for International Peace with the purpose of promoting peace by working with the intellectual elite and government leaders of other countries. Carnegie set up a ten-million-dollar fund to further the goals of the organization. Much of the fund consisted of stockholdings in United States Steel. (When World War I started in 1914, the stock's value increased astronomically due to sales related to arms production.)

In 1912 the NYPS merged with the APS. By 1914 sixty-three antiwar organizations were active in the United States. In most of these, particularly the larger ones, women did not have leadership roles. For this reason they formed the Woman's Peace Party in 1915.

The Woman's Peace Party combined antiwar principles and women's suffrage as issues. As the European war progressed, with U.S. entry into the war becoming an increasing possibility, the Woman's Peace Party split. Many women continued to campaign for the right to vote while proclaiming that their patriotism took precedence over antiwar sentiments.

Jeannette Rankin's patriotism followed a different course. Rankin had been legislative secretary of the

*A Montana Republican, Jeannette Rankin was a leading antiwar activist in the U.S. Congress. She voted against declaring war on Germany in 1917 (and later on, in 1941).*

National American Woman Suffrage Association before becoming the first woman in the history of the United States to serve in the House of Representatives. In 1917, when the House voted 373 to 50 to declare war against Germany, Rankin sided with the minority, declaring that, "I want to stand by my country, but I cannot vote for war. I vote No."

# THE PEOPLE'S COUNCIL OF AMERICA

The United States entered World War I in April 1917. In May President Wilson signed the Selective Service Act, which made ten million men between the ages of twenty-one and thirty eligible to serve in the war against Germany. Wilson had been reelected president on the promise that the United States would remain neutral. "There is such a thing," he had vowed, "as a nation being too proud to fight." He had changed his mind when German submarines sank American merchant ships carrying war supplies to Britain and France. He said, we must fight a war "to make the world safe for democracy," a war "to end all wars."

As the draft went into effect, a new antiwar organization, the People's Council of America, launched its campaign at New York City's Madison Square Garden. Over twenty thousand people attended. The People's Council was decidedly leftist. It "denounced war profiteering, insisted on adequate wages for labor," and advocated that U.S. soldiers follow the examples of Russian revolutionaries who had laid down their arms rather than go into battle against German and Austrian working men.

Some historians suggest that the People's Council at its peak had some two million sympathizers. Others believe that is an exaggeration. What is true, however, is that the People's Council attracted followers that the established peace organizations had neglected. Those groups had based their membership exclusively on "middle and upper classes," who, their leaders assumed, "could more easily understand and identify with the civilized quality of their move-ment than the unenlightened masses."

Recruitment of African Americans was also, for the most part, neglected by antiwar groups. Nevertheless, black intellectuals, includ-ing A. Philip Randolph, head of the Brotherhood of Sleeping Car Porters, published an antiwar periodical called the *Messenger*. In the *Atlantic Monthly*, African American author and lecturer W. E. B. DuBois described the European conflict as a war for empire, by which he meant domination over African colonies with their gold, diamonds, ivory, and other riches.

## THE ESPIONAGE ACT OF 1917

Soon after the United States entered the war, Congress passed and President Wilson signed the Espionage Act of 1917. It made it a crime to "obstruct recruiting and enlistment efforts." Eugene Debs was one of the first people to be charged under the act. Debs had been the Socialist Party candidate for president in four elections. He was under arrest for making speeches against the war in which he told young men that "you need to know that you are fit for some-thing better than slavery and cannon fodder."

Debs was convicted and sentenced to ten years in prison. The con-viction was appealed. In 1919, after the war had ended, the convic-tion was upheld by the Supreme Court of the United States. The reason, as summed up by Justice Oliver Wendell Holmes Jr. in another antiwar case of the period, was that, "when a nation is at war, many things that might be said in time of peace are such a hin-drance to its effort that their utterance will not be endured." Debs went to prison. In 1920, while still there, he ran for president one more time and received almost one million votes. In 1921 President Warren Harding pardoned Debs, and he was set free.

At the time that Debs was first charged, the Sedition Act had been passed. It made it a crime to speak or write "anything intended to cause contempt and scorn for the government of the United States, the Constitution, the flag, or the uniform of the armed forces; or to say or write anything urging interference with defense production." Before the war ended, between the Espionage Act and the Sedition Act, over nine hundred antiwar advocates were prosecuted, convicted, and jailed.

Among them was Robert Goldstein, producer of the silent film *The Spirit of '76.* He had started production in 1916 and completed the film just as the United States was entering the war. It was meant to be a patriotic epic dealing with the American Revolution. *Spirit* presented scenes of the signing of the Declaration of Independence, Valley Forge, and Patrick Henry's speech declaring for liberty or death. It also showed scenes of atrocities committed by British redcoats on colonial civilians.

Government censors ordered Goldstein to remove those scenes or risk prosecution. At first, he complied, but then he sneaked the censored scenes back into the film. Goldstein was charged under the Espionage Act and convicted. Federal District judge Benjamin Bledsoe justified the verdict on the basis that "we are engaged in a war in which Great Britain is an ally of the United States." He added that the film's purpose was to "incite hatred of England and England's soldiers," concluding that, "Great Britain, as an ally of ours, is working with us to fight the battle which we think strikes at our very existence as a nation." This was judged to be treason, and Goldstein was fined five thousand dollars and sentenced to ten years in prison. He served only three.

## PARANOIA AND PACIFISM

Despite the threat of prosecution, the Socialist Party continued to oppose the war. During the summer of 1917, antiwar Socialist meetings in Minnesota and Wisconsin drew thousands of people "in places," according to the *Plymouth Review* of Plymouth, Wisconsin, "where ordinarily a few hundred are considered large assemblages." According to the conservative *Beacon-Journal* of Akron, Ohio, "were an election to come now a mighty tide of socialism would inundate the Middle West." It added that the nation had "never embarked upon a more unpopular war."

During World War I, the antiwar message of the Socialist Party attracted thousands of new members. However, even before the war began, its rhetoric and programs, along with those of other antiwar organizations regarded as leftist, had alarmed the Department of Justice. They had taken to heart Lenin's resolution adopted by the Socialist International to exploit the war "to hasten the abolition of capitalism." They were alarmed by hearing echoes of it in antiwar speeches.

The Justice Department reacted by sponsoring the American Protective League to expose and combat subversive activities. By June 1917, only two months after the United States entered the war, the

*This painting captures the brutal fighting during World War I. As a result of the high casualties, antiwar sentiments increased throughout the United States.*

league had amassed a membership of nearly one hundred thousand people, with chapters in six hundred American cities. The membership was made up of "the leading men in their communities." These civic leaders eventually claimed to have identified an astounding three million cases of disloyalty throughout the nation.

Events in Russia added to the growing popular fear of subversion in the United States. The bloodiness of the Bolshevik Revolution and the assassination of the czar and his wife and children caused grave concern. Russia's signing of a separate armistice with Germany at Brest Litovsk on December 15, 1917, fed the fires of suspicion of American Socialists, union leaders, and radicals of every stripe. These concerns—mounting to what many historians consider hysterical proportions after World War I—were one of the conflict's two main legacies. The other, a reaction to the appalling total of ten million soldiers killed in the war, created a sentiment for pacifism that would dominate U.S. policy toward the world for the next twenty years.

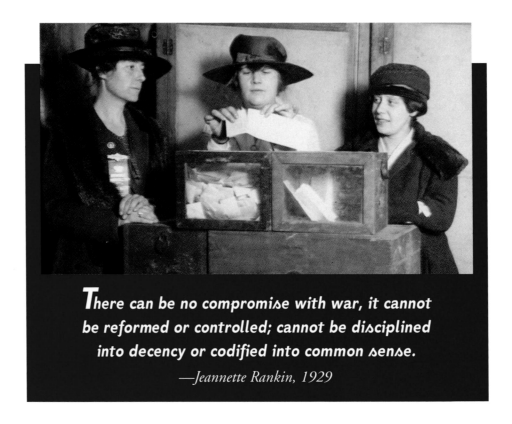

*There can be no compromise with war, it cannot be reformed or controlled; cannot be disciplined into decency or codified into common sense.*
—*Jeannette Rankin, 1929*

# REMEMBER PEARL HARBOR!

In the aftermath of World War I, the Nineteenth Amendment to the Constitution gave American women the right to vote, and many suffragist activists turned to other issues. Antiwar movements attracted them in great numbers. Some of these were devoted solely to peace, while some embraced a variety of causes, including poverty, slum clearance, labor issues, immigrant rights, antifascism, and others.

## THE WOMEN'S PEACE SOCIETY

The different approaches split apart the New York City Woman's Peace Party. It had been formed with the belief that mothers have "a more intimate sense of the value of human life," which gave them unique qualifications to protest war. In 1919 a majority of the organization's executive committee resigned because they felt that the party should focus solely on putting an end to war, rather than dissipating its energies on other issues. They organized the Women's Peace Society (WPS) and elected seventy-five-year-old Fanny Garrison Villard as its permanent chairperson. Fanny Villard was the only daughter of William Lloyd Garrison and had been active in the peace movement throughout World War I.

Absolute opposition to war, with no exceptions, was the program of the WPS. To join, a woman had only to sign the pledge and pay

*Fanny Villard* (center) *displays her antiwar sentiments on her car as well as on her person.*

twenty-five cents in dues. WPS spokesperson and lawyer Elinor Byrns summed up what that meant. Members must promise to oppose violence even in such just causes as "preserving law and order, or defending liberty and property, or . . . securing the safety of women and children." A WPS resolution insisted that "women should not want rights, privileges or protection secured for them at the cost of men's lives." Lobbying lawmakers over such issues as the 1919 naval armaments race between the United States, Britain, and Japan was a main activity of the WPS.

## THE PALMER RAIDS

Meanwhile, those left in the New York City Woman's Peace Party had joined the national Woman's Peace Party, which eventually became the U.S. branch of the Women's International League for Peace and Freedom (WILPF). This organization worked toward world peace, economic freedom, and legal equality. Unlike the WPS, however, nonresistance was not part of its philosophy.

Both these women's peace organizations occupied a sort of middle ground between the Carnegie Endowment for International Peace on the right and the People's Council of America on the left. Yet when the People's Council and the Socialist Party were targeted by the attorney general of the United States as Communist sympathizers, the women's peace groups were lumped together with them. In the anti-Communist hysteria, well-known peace advocates of the WILPF, such as social worker and reformer Jane Addams and immigrant advocate Lillian Wald, were branded as "radicals."

The anti-Communist hysteria had escalated on June 2, 1919, when a bomb set off in Washington, D.C., shattered the homes of several top government officials, including that of Attorney General A. Mitchell Palmer. The men who exploded the bomb were blown to bits. They were widely believed to be Bolshevik anarchists. When strikes and labor violence across the country followed, they sparked

*Crowds gathered in June 1919 to view the devastation outside the bombed-out home of Attorney General A. Mitchell Palmer. The bombers were believed to be Bolshevik anarchists.*

the so-called Palmer Raids to round up foreign-born subversives and deport them. The focus was on aliens, but it quickly encompassed many who had international ties in the various peace organizations. Connections with peace movements in other countries were automatically suspect. Some American peace organization offices were raided, their files confiscated, and various members held for questioning. Members not born in the United States faced deportation. The Palmer Raids continued throughout the early 1920s.

## THE KELLOGG-BRIAND PACT

At the time the Palmer Raids were getting under way, the administration of President Woodrow Wilson was fighting a losing battle for the United States to join the League of Nations. The league had been conceived by Wilson and gained approval in Europe at the end of the war. But antiwar feeling in the United States had hardened into a determination not to be embroiled in European affairs lest such involvement lead America into another war. While some peace groups regarded the league as an opportunity to draft an international code that would ban war, the powerful Carnegie Endowment for International Peace did not endorse the league.

Because it was conservative and backed by prominent leaders in the fields of industry, banking, and education, the Carnegie Endowment had been able to establish a close relationship with the State Department. It might ignore other peace groups—particularly under the Republican administrations that succeeded Wilson throughout the 1920s—but the spokespersons of the Carnegie Endowment had both access and powers of persuasion. They were able to help shape and influence the signing of the Kellogg-Briand Pact of 1928 in which sixty-three nations, including the United States, renounced war as an instrument of national policy.

French foreign minister Aristide Briand and U.S. secretary of state Frank B. Kellogg were the two men who drew up the pact that was named after them. As the representative of a nation that had been ravaged by World War I, Briand first suggested a nonaggression pact. Kellogg, an isolationist, was prodded into negotiations by strong antiwar sentiment in the United States. Although the negotiations resulted in several loopholes in the Kellogg-Briand Pact, Kellogg was awarded the Nobel Peace Prize in 1929.

The Kellogg-Briand Pact echoed "The World Petition to Prevent War Between Nations" presented to the second Hague Peace Conference in 1907. The petition had been the work of Anna B. Eckstein, the vice president of the APS at that time. Born in Germany, Eckstein had emigrated to the United States and had become an American citizen. She had collected two million signatures for the petition she presented at The Hague. It asked the heads of the forty-four nations represented at the conference to pledge to "adjust all international interests by treaty, and by arbitration

*Anna Eckstein's contribution to the peace movement was eventually to collect six million signatures on an antiwar petition. This feat was especially amazing for a woman in the first decade of the twentieth century.*

reduce the necessity of armaments." An economic boycott by the other nations would penalize any country's failure to keep the pledge. An international court of arbitration would settle conflicts of interest among countries.

Although the 1907 Hague Conference did not act on the petition, Anna Eckstein was encouraged by the many positive responses she received from individual delegates. Over the next seven years, she collected a total of six million signatures for her peace petition. She intended to present it to the third Hague Peace Conference, but World War I broke out and the conference was canceled. The blow, combined with her always frail health, brought on a nervous breakdown. However, Eckstein's work had impressed some of the more conservative and influential men in the peace movement, and through them her work played a part in the wording of the 1928 Kellogg-Briand Pact.

## THE BONUS MARCH

The Kellogg-Briand Pact was flawed. And this became all too clear during the years leading up to World War II (1939–1945). These were difficult years for the world and for the United States. A year after Kellogg-Briand was signed, the stock market crashed. The chaos of the Great Depression (1929–1942) swept over America and the world.

By 1932 one-third of the nation was ill fed, ill clothed, and ill housed. Between eleven million and fifteen million people were out of work. Unemployed World War I veterans demanded help in the form of a bonus for their military service. Congress had voted to give them the bonus but had delayed paying it. Twenty thousand veterans marched on Washington, D.C., and set up Hoovervilles—groups of tin-and-tarpaper shanties named after President Herbert Hoover, who insisted that "conditions are fundamentally sound." They announced that they were going

*A ragged one-thousand-man army of ex-soldiers rally forces in New York's Union Square as they prepare to march to Washington, D.C. in 1932. The marchers were renewing their demands for the payment of the veterans' bonus and were protesting against the cuts in veterans' disability funds.*

to stay until the bonus was paid. On July 28, 1932, acting on President Hoover's orders, federal troops armed with machine guns and tear gas set fire to the shanties. One veteran was killed, and several others were injured. The veterans were driven out of Washington.

The bitterness engendered by the treatment of the bonus marchers was widespread. The veterans, their families, their friends, and hundreds of thousands of other Americans regarded it as a betrayal of those who had fought and died in World War I. The war itself was questioned. The world had not been made safe for democracy. There was no democracy in Germany or Russia or Japan or many other countries. A feeling swept over the nation that American boys must never again risk their lives in a foreign war. This was not the traditional pacifism of peace groups, not the antiviolence of Quakers or humanists. This was isolationism.

## THE ISOLATIONISTS

A group of powerful senators championed isolationism. Leading them was the chairperson of the influential Senate Foreign Relations Committee, Republican William E. Borah of Idaho. Following World War I, Borah had led the successful opposition to

*Idaho Republican senator William E. Borah was the antiwar movement's strongest advocate during his thirty-three years in office.*

U.S. participation in the League of Nations and its World Court. Throughout the 1930s, "the Lion of Idaho," as he was known, fought every attempt to modernize the U.S. military, increase its budgets, or build up its manpower reserves. Borah, who was elected to the Senate five times and served a total of thirty-three years, supported several antiwar bills in keeping with the aims of the various peace organizations.

During the first term of Democratic president Franklin D. Roosevelt, Borah led a powerful antiwar bloc of conservative and liberal senators. The group included Hiram Johnson of California, Robert La Follette of Wisconsin, George Norris of Nebraska, Arthur Vandenberg of Michigan, Bennett Champ Clark of Missouri, and Gerald P. Nye of North Dakota. In 1934 Senator Nye presided over hearings of a special Senate committee investigating the munitions industry. The committee "dug up sensational evidence . . . that the munitions interests had successfully outwitted the government by getting around embargoes placed . . . on the export of war materials to belligerent countries." Nye's committee found proof of "excessive profits" amassed by "the salesmen of death."

Such revelations outraged the nation. The ranks of isolationists multiplied. Antiwar groups, particularly the WILPF, campaigned for the first Neutrality Act, which would forbid arms shipments to countries at war.

Senators Nye and Vandenberg, after consulting with various peace activists on the wording, introduced the bill, and the Senate passed it. President Roosevelt, who in general favored building up the armed forces, went along with overwhelming public approval of the bill and signed it into law in September 1935.

Six months later, on February 29, 1936, a second Neutrality Act became law. It was followed by a third Neutrality Act enacted in 1937. These banned making loans to nations that waged war. The acts said the nation could buy non-war-related goods for cash only and only if they transported them in their own ships.

## THE COMMUNIST CONFLICTS

As well as being isolationist, the pro-peace senators were strongly anti-Communist. They were beyond being accused of Bolshevik sympathies. This was not, however, true of some of the antiwar organizations.

The American branch of the Fellowship of Reconciliation (FOR), which had begun as part of an international Christian pacifist movement originating in Britain, had attracted many leftists following World War I. A faction had formed that was friendly to the Soviet Union. This faction believed that violence was justifiable when combating the evils of capitalism. A schism developed among the members, and, to deal with it, they were asked, "Should the FOR hold on to non-violence in the class war as well as in international war?" The response was 877 yes to 97 no.

The FOR further rejected violence with a declaration of noncooperation with Communists. This brought them into conflict with a new peace organization, the American League against War and Fascism, which supported Soviet foreign policy. "Communists have nothing but contempt for religion and for pacifism," declared vice chairman of FOR Kirby Page, adding that they used cooperation with peace organizations as "a means of boring from within." Nevertheless, two years after its founding in 1933, the American League against War and Fascism had a membership of over two million people. Much of this was due to affiliations with organizations in organized labor.

## MAJOR PACIFIST MOVEMENTS

In the mid-1930s, concern that the peace movement might be co-opted by the Left led a group of prominent American leaders to organize the Emergency Peace Campaign. This coalition of antiwar groups drew its membership mostly from the middle and upper classes. Many historians regard the Emergency Peace Campaign as the greatest single pacifist effort of the period between the two world wars. Its main thrust was isolationist, and its first effort was the Neutrality Campaign, which focused on building public support for legislation that would firm up U.S. resistance to foreign entanglements. On April 6, 1937, as the possibility of a major war in Europe was building, the Emergency Peace Campaign launched a No-Foreign-War Crusade designed to increase and publicize the determination of the American people not to be drawn into such a conflict. The crusade exerted great influence over local and federal politicians. At its peak, the Emergency Peace Campaign had committees operating in two thousand U.S. cities and towns. Its list of prominent supporters included Admiral Richard E. Byrd and First Lady Eleanor Roosevelt. The impact of the Emergency Peace Campaign was intensified by the actions of peace groups whose positions its leaders rejected.

Chief among these efforts were 1930s student antiwar movements. Several liberal organizations—the National Student Federation of America, the American Youth Congress, the Socialist League for Industrial Democracy, and the Communist-influenced National Student League—led the way. These groups joined together to hold an annual student strike against war. They pledged "not to support the government of the United States in any war it may conduct." At their peak, the student strikes involved half a million students.

The large numbers of people actively involved in antiwar activities, combined with the powerful isolationist faction in Congress, had a sustained effect on U.S. public opinion. A majority of citizens opposed any military intervention in foreign conflicts. This was the atmosphere as war clouds gathered over Europe.

## DAY OF INFAMY

In defiance of American public opinion, President Roosevelt's War Department gave out contracts for the largest orders of military equipment in U.S. history on August 10, 1939. Three weeks later, the Nazis invaded Poland, and World War II began. Roosevelt, contradicting his widely criticized preparedness program, proclaimed U.S. neutrality in the war. He announced an embargo on arms shipments and all military equipment to all those countries in which "a state of war unhappily exists." This included France, Germany, Britain, Poland, India, Australia, and New Zealand. Less than two months later, Roosevelt approved a joint congressional resolution lifting the embargo.

His efforts signaled the beginning of a series of moves designed to get the United States ready for war. The antiwar movement understood this and reacted. As war broke out abroad, a group of organizations including the FOR, the WILPF, the War Resisters League, the American Friends Service Committee, and others published a book entitled *How to Keep America Out of War.* At the same time, isolationist

*Polish citizens render the Nazi salute as German cavalry troops enter Lodz, Poland, early in World War II.*

Republicans opposed to President Roosevelt were forming the America First Committee to oppose any military buildup that would lead to U.S. entry into the war. When the German American Bund, an anti-Semitic and pro-Nazi militia-style organization, began attending its meetings in groups, America First was compromised and lost much public support.

The Bund was financed by the Nazi Party of German chancellor Adolf Hitler. Following the principles laid down in Hitler's book *Mein Kampf,* the Germans were already murdering political opponents and Jews in the countries they invaded. Bund members in New York and other cities were beating up Jews and other minorities. When American aviator-hero Charles Lindbergh, the first person to fly nonstop across the Atlantic Ocean, attended a Bund meeting, the America First Committee, which he strongly supported, was tarnished by his disgrace.

Mounting U.S. anti-Nazi sentiment worked against all of the various antiwar efforts. On June 22, 1940, France surrendered to the

*Charles Lindbergh speaks to supporters of the isolationist group, America First, in the 1930s.*

Nazis. That summer, Congress appropriated nearly $16 billion to create a huge air force and a two-ocean navy. The army's chief of staff, General George C. Marshall, called for a military force of two million men. Despite a protest to the House Military Affairs Committee by antiwar groups to "Keep our U.S. out of war and keep conscription out of our U.S.," the first peacetime draft in U.S. history went into effect on October 29, 1940.

That fall, President Roosevelt was reelected to a third term. On December 29, 1940, in a radio broadcast to the nation, he announced his administration's intention of making the United States an "arsenal of democracy" to supply the forces fighting Nazism. In March 1941, Congress authorized Lend Lease, a program that "gave the president the authority to aid any nation whose defense he believed vital to the U.S." Isolationists in the Senate had opposed the measure. Ohio senator Robert A. Taft had called Lend Lease the road to war, claiming it "would plow under every fourth American boy." However, the isolationist senators were no longer powerful enough to stand up to the preparedness policies of the administration.

On December 7, 1941, the Sunday that President Roosevelt called a "day which will live in infamy," the Japanese bombed Pearl Harbor in the Hawaiian Islands. The attack killed two thousand sailors and four hundred civilians. Another thirteen hundred Americans were wounded. The Japanese seriously damaged five battleships and fourteen smaller ships and destroyed two hundred military planes.

Congress immediately declared war on Japan. Only one no vote was heard in Congress. Montana congresswoman Jeannette Rankin voiced it. She stood alone, reviled, faithful to her antiwar principles despite her awareness that she was ending her political career. Not many members of peace organizations stood with her. The United States had been attacked, and like most Americans, they rallied around the flag. The cause of peace was a casualty of Japanese bombs. The antiwar organizations had been shattered for the duration, their

*Black smoke rises from the burning wrecks of several U.S. Navy battleships. A Japanese surprise attack on Pearl Harbor on the Hawaiian island of Oahu, on December 7, 1941, destroyed many ships.*

dwindling membership rendered ineffectual as the nation went to war. The slogan had become "Remember Pearl Harbor!" The peace movement had no words to compete with the sentiment.

## BAN THE BOMB

On July 16, 1945, scientists successfully detonated the world's first atomic bomb in the New Mexico desert. Leo Szilard, one of the scientists who had helped develop it, witnessed the explosion. He concluded that the bomb should not be dropped on people and wrote a petition that sixty-nine other atomic scientists signed. It warned that, if the United States dropped the bomb, it would begin an era of unimaginable destruction. The signers constituted the most important antiwar effort of World War II, but their efforts were too late.

A U.S. plane dropped the first atomic bomb on Hiroshima, Japan, on Monday, August 6, 1945. It killed 200,000 people. A second atomic bomb was dropped on Nagasaki, Japan, on August 9, killing 140,000. These events ended the war in the Pacific.

Six months later, Joseph Stalin—leader of the Communist Soviet Union, a wartime ally of the capitalist United States—declared that peace was impossible until Communism replaced capitalism. His speech kicked off the Cold War (1945–1991) that pitted the Soviet Union and its supporters against the United States and its allies. The U.S. government ordered a loyalty check of federal employees and

*Rubble was all that was left after the explosion of an atomic bomb in Hiroshima, Japan, on August 6, 1945. The bombing of Hiroshima and Nagasaki accomplished the stated goal of ending the war with Japan, but at a terrible cost.*

fired people who had Communist connections. Suddenly, Americans who had supported the Soviet Union during the war found themselves under suspicion.

In 1950 the Soviet Union detonated its first nuclear bomb. The two archenemies both had weapons of mass destruction and were well on their way to being able to deliver them from long distances. This might've been the time for the old-line peace organizations to raise their voices, but they didn't. The fears inspired by newspapers and by anti-Communist groups—such as the House Un-American Activities Committee and the Senate Internal Security Subcommittee—had silenced them.

By the mid-1950s, fear of Communism was replaced with fear of nuclear annihilation. Both the United States and the Soviet Union had developed a hydrogen bomb, which was many times more powerful than the atomic bomb. Both nations were manufacturing long-range rockets to carry nuclear weapons. Children were learning "duck-and-cover" techniques in schools to shield them in the event of a nuclear attack. Their parents were building fallout shelters. Fear was widespread. The feeling was that something must be done to avoid a confrontation that could result in mass destruction.

In 1957 leading U.S. pacifists founded the National Committee for a Sane Nuclear Policy (SANE). The group put an ad in the *New York Times,* calling for an immediate end to nuclear testing. The response was overwhelming. Within six months, SANE had 130 chapters around the country. The organization gathered thousands of signatures urging a nuclear test ban and presented them at the 1958–1959 Geneva conference on disarmament. SANE organized "Ban the Bomb" rallies across the country that attracted thousands, including celebrities like Eleanor Roosevelt, Martin Luther King Jr., Dr. Benjamin Spock, and Marlon Brando.

The antinuclear movement kept growing in the early 1960s, and the voices of the protesters were heard and got results. In 1963, bowing to worldwide public opinion, the United States, the Soviet

*Women Strike for Peace representatives carry placards outside the United Nations headquarters in New York City, where the UN Security Council met to discuss the 1962 Cuban Missile Crisis.*

Union, and Britain signed the first nuclear test ban treaty. It forbid aboveground testing of bombs that caused nuclear fallout. Many anti-war activists were hoping it was the beginning of a race for peace.

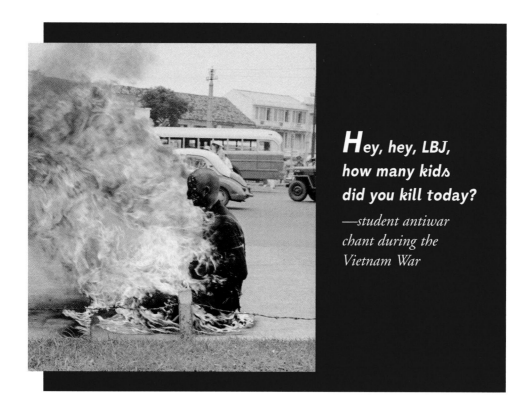

# THE QUAGMIRE

It has been said that Vietnam was the first war to be fought on television. In reality, it was fought in the jungles and rice paddies, the deltas and air space of Southeast Asia. However, the TV images—the naked child fleeing the napalm blast, the South Vietnamese officer pressing his pistol to the temple of a prisoner and firing, a Buddhist monk dousing himself with gasoline and setting himself aflame—brought the reality of war home with an impact that was new to America. The images swelled the ranks of those who opposed the conflict, creating the largest and most vocal antiwar movement in U.S. history.

## STRANGE BEDFELLOWS

The movement was made up of many diverse elements. Historian Howard Zinn writes that, "some of the first signs of opposition to the Vietnam war came out of the civil rights movement." Young African Americans who had fought for civil rights during the late 1950s and early 1960s did not believe that black men should fight in a white man's war in Vietnam while still being denied equality in Mississippi and Alabama. Nobel Prize-winning civil rights leader Dr. Martin Luther King Jr. spoke out against the war and led marches in opposition to it. (Some African Americans felt he should not have diverted his energy and prestige from the civil rights struggle.) Heavyweight boxing champion Muhammad Ali, who had marched for civil rights, was stripped of his title and sentenced to five years in prison for refusing to be drafted into the military.

*Former world heavyweight boxing champion Muhammad Ali—then known as Cassius Clay* (left)*—leaves federal court in 1967 after an all-white jury found him guilty on charges of refusing to be inducted into the U.S. armed forces.*

"I cannot be true to my belief in my religion by accepting such a call," he said. African American Dick Gregory, long a civil rights activist, defied the State Department and went to Vietnam to entertain U.S. prisoners of war (POWs).

Priests and nuns who had fought for civil rights organized the Catholic Peace Fellowship to protest U.S. actions in Vietnam. Old left and new left organizations with radical agendas, various professional groups and citizens' groups, ministers and rabbis, students and flower children, hippies and Yippies became part of the anti-Vietnam War movement. Women Strike for Peace marched alongside activist Students for a Democratic Society (SDS). SANE demonstrated with the Black Panthers. Clergy and Laymen Concerned About Vietnam (CALCAV) joined protests that included the Communist Party. Serious Socialists joined with prankster Yippies to protest the war. Groups that were sometimes in active opposition to one another's principles and tactics put aside their differences.

They were brought together by the Mobe, a leadership committee from a broad range of peace groups ranging from the Quakers to the Communist Party. The committee members changed from event to event as the leadership reconstituted itself, but always the aim was to make a variety of groups embracing various philosophies and tactics demonstrate together against the war. In 1966 came the first Spring Mobilization and then the Student Mobilization. In 1967 came the National Mobilization and, in 1969, the New Mobilization.

## THE DOMINO THEORY

What was this war they were opposing? Why were we in Vietnam? Vietnam was a French colony before World War II. Following the war, Communist rebels had ousted the French from North Vietnam. South Vietnam, however, had not fallen under Communist rule. In 1954 the Geneva Accords divided Vietnam at the 17th parallel. Communists controlled the area north of the line. Anti-Communists, backed by both the French and the United States, were in charge south of the line. Elections to reunify the country were scheduled for 1956. When the leadership of South Vietnam refused to participate in the elections, U.S. secretary of state John Foster Dulles decided that the United States should not "make the slightest effort to" have them held. This refusal to reunify the country led to a rebellion in South Vietnam by the National Liberation Front (NLF), also known as the Vietcong. The north backed the NLF and provided it with arms, training, and eventually massive military support.

The Soviet Union and China also supported the NLF as part of Communism's worldwide struggle against capitalism. The leaders of both nations had asserted that capitalism must be destroyed. Soviet premier Nikita Khrushchev put it bluntly: "We will bury you!"

A U.S. National Security Council document pointed out that

*By the mid-1950s, after the war with France, much of Vietnam lay in ruins. The Soviet Union and China—the world's two largest Communist nations— supported North Vietnam in its effort to subdue South Vietnam.*

"Communist control of all of Southeast Asia would . . . seriously jeopardize fundamental U.S. security interests in the Far East." Malaysia, Indonesia, the Philippines, New Guinea, perhaps even Australia and Hawaii would be at risk. That was the domino theory.

President Eisenhower sent military advisers to help South Vietnam defend itself. Under President Kennedy, their number grew to sixteen thousand. In January 1962, Kennedy added two army divisions.

## THE GULF OF TONKIN RESOLUTION

In August 1964, Vietnamese patrol boats attacked two U.S. destroyers allegedly on routine patrol in the Gulf of Tonkin off the coast of North Vietnam. Congress was told that the attack had taken place in neutral waters and was unprovoked. In response to a request by President Lyndon Johnson, Congress passed the Gulf of Tonkin Resolution giving him the power to take any action necessary to oppose North Vietnamese aggression. Later, it was revealed that the two U.S. ships had been aiding South Vietnamese military operations against the North Vietnamese.

The Gulf of Tonkin Resolution later gave authority for the

*President Johnson* (seated) *announces the Gulf of Tonkin Resolution in 1964.*

buildup of U.S. troops in Vietnam to a total of 540,000. Altogether, 2.7 million men and women would eventually serve in Vietnam. Almost sixty thousand would give their lives. More than three hundred thousand would be wounded.

As these numbers accumulated, sentiment against the war was growing in America. Not yet coordinated by the Mobe, many protests occurred, some by small groups and a few individuals. Two of these actions were tragic.

In November 1965, a thirty-two-year-old Quaker, Norman Morrison, the father of three children, set himself on fire in front of the Pentagon entrance in Washington, D.C. His one-year-old daughter was in his arms as his clothes caught fire. She was snatched to safety by a passerby as Morrison went up in flames. Morrison's wife said he was upset about the loss of life in Vietnam. A week later, Roger LaPorte of the Catholic Worker movement set himself on fire outside the United Nations in protest against the war. That same month, the media reported that a large rally in Washington had attracted "as many mothers, fathers and professionals as there were students protesting the Vietnam War."

## STUDENT ANTIWAR MOVEMENT

College students and even some high school students filled the ranks of the antiwar movement. They were in the forefront in March 1966 when protest marches were held by thousands of people—twenty thousand in New York alone—in major cities throughout the country. Not all students, however, opposed the war. In New York, protesters were pelted with eggs by pro-war students, and in Boston they were attacked by high school students.

Nevertheless, by May 1966, antiwar protests were sweeping the campuses and growing more violent. Reserve Officers' Training Corps (ROTC) recruitment on campus further infuriated antiwar students who viewed it as a tool to enlist more soldiers for Vietnam. Students seized control of the administration offices at the University of Chicago and obstructed classroom teaching at City College in New York.

Hordes of students flocked to Washington in October 1967, as fifty thousand protesters marched on the Pentagon. They were met with rifles and bayonets. The media reported that "many of the demonstrators were bashed over the head with nightsticks and rifle butts" and "blood dripped on the sidewalk." About two hundred fifty protesters were arrested, including novelist Norman Mailer and peace activist David Dellinger, at that time chairman of the Mobe. Dellinger had played a major role in organizing the rally.

## PROTESTING THE DRAFT

Most of the male students involved in such actions were exempted from the draft because they were in school. Other young men dealt with the draft in different ways. Some enlisted because they believed that by so doing they could get a better deal. Others waited, hoping that the lottery system by which the draft operated would not result in their number being called. Still others fled to Canada and other countries. Some took a stand against the war and publicly burned their draft cards.

Many who were too old to be drafted took other actions to protest the selective service system. Middle-aged people were prominent in a two-day protest to block the draft center in New York City. Mounted police trampled protesters and used their billy clubs to thump skulls. Over five hundred forty people were arrested, among them famous pediatrician Dr. Benjamin Spock.

Dr. Spock and the Reverend William Sloane Coffin Jr., had "distributed and caused to be distributed . . . a statement entitled 'A Call to Resist Illegitimate Authority,'" meaning the draft. On October 20, 1967, the pair entered the Justice Department and "abandoned a fabricoid briefcase" containing draft cards. On January 5, 1968, a federal Grand Jury returned an indictment charging Spock, Coffin, and three others with conspiring to "sponsor and support a nation-wide program of resistance" to the draft. Dr. Spock and the Reverend Coffin were subsequently convicted, but the U.S. Court of Appeals later overturned the convictions.

Others opposed the draft using more extreme measures. Father Philip Berrigan and Thomas Lewis of Artists Concerned about Vietnam broke into the Selective Service headquarters in Baltimore and poured duck blood over draft files. Father Berrigan called the act "sacrificial and constructive." The judge who sentenced the two men said they were attempting to "bring down this society."

Prominent women also emerged as leaders of the antiwar movement. Prize-winning author Grace Paley led one group that blocked the New York City induction center, locking arms with fellow protesters as the mounted police charged them. Folk singers Judy Collins and Buffy Sainte-Marie entertained without pay at countless rallies. Movie star Jane Fonda traveled to North Vietnam to voice her protest against U.S. involvement in the war. Criticized for a lack of patriotism, she was reviled as "Hanoi Jane."

*Jane Fonda* (center) *became "Hanoi Jane" after she visited Hanoi in North Vietnam and supported the country's effort to win the Vietnam War.*

## ASSASSINATION AND RIOT

By 1968 the demonstrations were ongoing, and their numbers were mounting. Young marchers were echoing organized hard-liners like the SDS and chanting "HEY, HEY, LBJ, HOW MANY BOYS DID YOU KILL TODAY?" Other marchers may have winced at the words, but the chants reflected the depth of bitterness toward Johnson.

In March 1968, Minnesota senator Eugene McCarthy, running on an antiwar platform, captured 40 percent of the vote in the New Hampshire Democratic Party primary. Johnson won the primary, but for an incumbent president, McCarthy's numbers were a devastating blow. On March 31, in a speech that stunned the nation, Johnson announced that because of "division in the American

*Anti-Vietnam War protesters march down New York City's Fifth Avenue in 1968.*

house," he would "not accept the nomination of my party as your president."

Tragedy followed. On April 4, Dr. Martin Luther King Jr. was assassinated. African Americans rioted in Harlem in New York.

At this time, Columbia University was fighting with Harlem community leaders over building a new gymnasium on property they claimed was badly needed for new housing. Columbia's large campus antiwar movement sided with the community. Shortly after King's murder, male and female students staged a sit-in at five Columbia buildings. The dean of the college was held hostage in his office for twenty-four hours. Protesters from Harlem thronged to Columbia to support the sit-in. Soon thousands of people were rioting on campus. Eventually, Columbia University president Dr. Grayson Kirk called in the police, and the crowd was dispersed. Many of those who staged the sit-in were arrested.

*In New York, Columbia University students protest the war in Vietnam in April of 1968. Police line the steps of the Low Memorial Library, one of five buildings that protesters continued to occupy during the sit-in.*

## THE GATHERING STORM

In June 1968, Robert Kennedy was assassinated in Los Angeles. Senator Kennedy had just won the California Democratic primary race for the presidential nomination on an anti–Vietnam War platform. Shaken by his death, the antiwar movement prepared for the Democratic National Convention scheduled to take place in Chicago in August.

Thousands of antiwar advocates gathered in Chicago. Some were organized by the Mobe, which was then led by Tom Hayden of the SDS. Some were young, neatly dressed McCarthy campaign workers. Others were Yippies, led by Abbie Hoffman who had recently gained media attention by throwing dollar bills from a balcony onto the floor of the New York Stock Exchange.

A majority of the demonstrators who came to Chicago wanted the convention to nominate Eugene McCarthy for president. Vice President Hubert Humphrey, favored by the polls to win the nomination, had supported the Vietnam War and was considered Johnson's candidate. The peace people also wanted the convention to pass a minority plank calling for "an immediate halt to the bombing of North Vietnam." Both objectives failed.

## "DUMP THE HUMP!"

Prior to the convention, requests for demonstrations and rallies had been turned down by the Chicago administration. Mayor Richard J. Daley had announced that "the city's 12,000 man police force would be placed on twelve-hour shifts during the week of the convention." Tension increased when Abbie Hoffman threatened to put the drug LSD in the reservoirs that provided Chicago's drinking water. Meant as a joke, it was an impossibility (too much LSD would have been required to have any effect), but Mayor Daley took it seriously. He announced that police would be armed with shotguns and that five thousand national guardsmen and six thousand army troops would be on call during the week of the convention.

*Chaos enveloped the city of Chicago during the 1968 Democratic National Convention. Here one of thousands of demonstrators falls to the pavement as he is pursued by Chicago police officers carrying nightsticks.*

On Sunday, August 25, protesters gathered in Lincoln Park. When police ordered them to leave, they chanted, "The parks belong to the people!" Preceded by a cloud of tear gas, the officers—some of whom had removed their badges to keep from being identified—began to club protesters and bystanders. Journalists and photographers covering the incident retreated to a traffic island outside the park. Suddenly, as if on order, the police turned and charged them, clubs swinging wildly.

The next day, the convention began. It was marked by bizarre incidents and violence. The lobby of the Conrad Hilton Hotel, where both Humphrey and McCarthy had their headquarters, gave off a sickening odor from stink bombs. When Hubert Humphrey arrived, shaking hands as he passed through the crowd, one man held onto his hand, shoved his face into Humphrey's, and screamed "Dump the Hump [a nickname for Humphrey]!" Later, inside the convention hall, two antiwar delegates were dragged from the floor by guards, and CBS correspondent Mike Wallace was punched in the face.

Roughly ten thousand protesters gathered for a rally in Grant Park opposite the Conrad Hilton Hotel on Wednesday, August 28. During the speeches, protesters tried to take down an American flag from a nearby pole. Police charged toward the flagpole. Demonstrators attempted to block them. An all-out police riot ensued, with many demonstrators and bystanders being clubbed unconscious.

## "THE WHOLE WORLD IS WATCHING"

On Thursday evening, Hubert Humphrey was nominated. Military jeeps jammed the streets between Grant Park and the convention center. Flatbed trucks were on hand with guns mounted on them. Tanks and additional members of the National Guard were also in evidence. When the demonstrators in Grant Park attempted to march to the convention, tear gas stopped them. A sultry wind wafted the gas over downtown Chicago, where much of it settled. Protesters regrouped in Grant Park. Some who had been hurt in scuffles with the police were given sanctuary in McCarthy headquarters in the Conrad Hilton. The police raided the headquarters and drove them out.

Rifles at the ready, members of the National Guard ringed Grant Park. Self-appointed leaders in the crowd of protesters led chants. Chanters locked arms and swayed toward them. Some of the National Guard—nervous, sweating in the hot night, bleary-eyed from the residue of tear gas—tentatively pointed their guns. The situation was defused when South Africa's bishop Desmond Tutu, who had earlier addressed the demonstrators, stepped in front of them and strode down the ranks of the National Guard, blessing each in turn. A while later a candlelight parade of peace delegates led by New York senator Paul O'Dwyer appeared, singing "America, the Beautiful."

In the wake of the convention, many blamed the leaders of the demonstrators for provoking violence. The leaders blamed government infiltrators. Indeed, CBS Television News reported that "about one demonstrator in six was an undercover agent." An official government investigation concluded that the Chicago police had themselves rioted. As they faced the billy clubs and the tear gas, the demonstrators had chanted, "The whole world is watching! The whole world is watching!" That was so, and in a way, that was their victory.

## SLAUGHTER ON CAMPUS

Two months later, President Johnson halted all air, naval, and artillery bombardment of North Vietnam. One of the demands of the Chicago protesters had been met. A few days later, Richard Nixon was elected president. In June 1969, President Nixon announced that twenty-five thousand troops were being brought home from Vietnam and that more troop withdrawals would follow. Also, peace talks began between North Vietnam and the United States and South Vietnam.

The peace talks bogged down. A major enemy offensive in Vietnam followed. Nixon warned that this would lead to a slowdown in the withdrawal of American forces. In Vietnam a company of men refused an order to go into battle. In November 1969, a quarter of a million people marched on Washington to protest the slowness of troop withdrawal. It was the largest gathering in the history of the antiwar movement.

Despite it, the war dragged on. A shocked America learned of the slaughter by U.S. soldiers of 567 villagers—infants, children, women, and elderly men—in the hamlet of My Lai in South Vietnam. President Nixon ordered thousands of U.S. troops into Cambodia to stop the infiltration of North Vietnamese soldiers fighting alongside the Vietcong. Campuses across the nation erupted with protests against the invasion. California governor Ronald Reagan recommended that "if it takes a bloodbath" to stop campus unrest, "then let's get it over with." On May 4, 1970, members of the National Guard called in to quell

*The 1970 shootings at Kent State shocked the world. This young woman's grief became a symbol of the antiwar movement.*

student disturbances at Kent State University in Ohio fired into a crowd, killing two female and two male students and wounding eight others. Some of the victims were onlookers not involved in the protest.

Ten days later, on May 14 to 15, students at all-black Jackson State College in Jackson, Mississippi, rallied to protest the Kent State killings. When police and state troopers arrived, they were jeered at, and some rocks were thrown. The officers warned the students to back off. When some of the students stayed put, the officers opened fire. One demonstrator was killed. A seventeen-year-old passerby, a high school student, was also killed. Twelve other protesters were struck by gunfire.

The killings prompted people who had never been part of the antiwar movement to demand an end to the violence. Revelations that the army and the CIA had been spying on thousands of Vietnam War opponents further shocked the nation. There was widespread agreement that a way out of Vietnam must be found.

On January 18, 1971, South Dakota senator George McGovern opened his campaign for the Democratic Party presidential nomination. He pledged that, if he was elected, he would withdraw all U.S. troops from Vietnam. Throughout the election campaign, the war dragged on. In April seven hundred Vietnam veterans discarded their medals and campaign ribbons at a rally in Washington, D.C. The following month, ten thousand antiwar protesters were arrested in the capital. Despite continuing demonstrations, in November 1972, President Nixon was reelected by an overwhelming majority.

A truce agreement was reached in Paris the following January. By March 29, the last U.S. troops had withdrawn from Vietnam and North Vietnam had released the last American prisoners of war that it acknowledged holding. However, this did not put an end to the Vietcong rebellion. In 1975 North Vietnamese and NLF troops converged on the capital city of Saigon. As the city fell, helicopters flew out the last Americans, embassy personnel, and others. That night, TV screens showed pictures of South Vietnamese making efforts to escape before the Communists took over.

*A few residents of Saigon managed to escape the 1975 Communist takeover by being airlifted by U.S. helicopters to ships off the Vietnamese coast.*

*W*e want justice!
We want peace!
U.S. out of the
Middle East!
—*antiwar chant
during the Iraqi wars*

# OPERATION IRAQI FREEDOM

**A**merican military involvement in the Vietnam War lasted eleven years. It was the longest war in American history. By contrast, combat operations in Iraq in 2003 were declared over by President George W. Bush forty-two days after the war started. It was a notably swift victory—although perhaps prematurely declared. Between these two events—the lengthy Vietnam War and the speedy Operation Iraqi Freedom—the strategies of peace changed.

## A VARIETY OF PROTESTS

In 1976 the National Peace Academy campaign was established. Its aim was to create a federally chartered institution for peacemaking and conflict resolution. By 1984 the campaign had forty-five thousand members. That year the U.S. Institute of Peace was established by Congress with a mandate to promote the prevention, management, and peaceful resolution of international conflicts.

Meanwhile, the antinuclear movement, which had been largely absorbed by the peace movement during the Vietnam War, had been reorganizing. On October 29, 1979, the fiftieth anniversary of the 1929 stock market crash, thousands of demonstrators chanting "No nukes!" linked arms and blocked entrances to the New York Stock Exchange. The action was aimed at investors in the nuclear industry that made weapons for war. It took 800 police officers to carry off the 1,045 demonstrators. In June 1982, 800,000 people rallied in New York City to demand an end to the nuclear arms race. A year later, the Roman Catholic bishops of the United States issued a pastoral letter urging all Catholics to exercise "the moral courage and technical means to say 'No' to an arms race."

Many professional groups organized during this period with the mission of spreading the word about the dangers of the nuclear arms race. These groups included Educators for Social Responsibility, Lawyers for Social Responsibility, and Physicians for Social Responsibility. They became part of the Nuclear Freeze campaign of the early 1980s. The campaign culminated in a gathering of one million people in New York City's Central Park in support of an end to nuclear testing. The *New York Times* called it the largest referendum on a single issue in the nation's history. The Nuclear Freeze campaign succeeded in placing a nuclear freeze resolution on statewide ballots across the country.

During the late 1970s and 1980s, a series of demonstrations took place in U.S. cities. They protested American training and arming of government and paramilitary forces in support of antireform

*With the Lincoln Memorial in the background, antiwar marchers cross the
Memorial Bridge in Washington, D.C., in 1981 on their way to the Pentagon
for a rally to protest U.S. involvement in El Salvador.*

movements in El Salvador and Nicaragua. Besides such old-line
peace organizations as the FOR and the AFSC, these protests
included actions by such new groups as Witness for Peace, the
Committee in Solidarity with the People of El Salvador (CISPES),
the Nicaraguan Support Network, and Pastors for Peace. Their
efforts involved establishing direct relationships with people in the
regions as well as educating the U.S. public as to their situation and
the reasons for it.

Protest rallies took place in 1983, when U.S. forces invaded the
tiny island of Grenada; in 1986, when American planes bombed the
base of Libyan dictator Muammar al-Qaddafi; and in 1989, when a
U.S. force of twenty-seven thousand troops invaded Panama. However,

in each case the military action was over too quickly for antiwar forces to organize effectively.

## THE GULF WAR

On August 2, 1990, dictator Saddam Hussein's Iraqi troops invaded the small country of Kuwait. Iraq claimed historical ownership of a large oil-rich area inside Kuwait, which exported oil to the United States. The UN Security Council rejected Iraq's claim and authorized military force against Iraq. Following this authorization, four hundred thousand U.S. soldiers were ordered to the Persian Gulf region. On January 17, 1991, U.S. warplanes began bombing Iraq.

Grassroots groups organized against the Gulf War. By the time the war was a week old, a call for a national antiwar mobilization brought out two hundred thousand people in Washington, D.C., and another one hundred thousand in San Francisco. Their chant was "No blood for oil!"

As antiwar coalitions were formed, rivalries developed. The National Campaign for Peace in the Middle East, while opposing U.S. military action, also demanded that Iraq pull out of Kuwait. The more radical International Action Center (IAC), with roots in the Socialist Workers Party, opposed this demand on the grounds that it lent legitimacy to U.S. military intervention. SANE supported sanctions against Iraq as an alternative to war. The National Network of Campuses against the War, formed in January 1991 by over one hundred college- and university-based antiwar committees, debated these issues within its ranks.

Former U.S. attorney general Ramsey Clark spoke out against the Gulf War. During the Vietnam War, Clark had been abhorred by peace activists for ordering the prosecution of Dr. Spock. Eventually, however, Clark had resigned as attorney general because he could no longer support the Vietnam War. During the Gulf War, Clark went to Iraq and observed the devastation caused by the dropping of eighty-eight thousand tons of U.S. bombs—the equivalent of seven atomic bombs in Hiroshima. He protested to the secretary general of the UN. "The scourge of war will never end if the United Nations tolerates this assault on life. The United Nations must not be an accessory to war crimes."

## SANCTIONS AND OVERSIGHT

Over the next twelve years, peace groups protested various actions involving Iraq. Prodded by the United States, the UN imposed severe sanctions on Iraq for violating the peace agreement ending the Gulf War. When the sanctions caused hardships, eventually resulting in more than one million deaths, half of them children under the age of five, peace groups campaigned to end them. An Oil-for-Food program—introduced by the UN with U.S. backing—was viewed by pacifists as inhumane, a means of providing America with fuel while doing little to alleviate the widespread starvation of the Iraqi people.

Much of their suffering, however, was the result of actions by Saddam's regime. In 1991 a rebellion by Shiite Muslims was put down brutally by Saddam's forces, which slaughtered entire village populations. Their remains would not be recovered from mass graves for twelve years. Saddam also used poison gas against Kurds seeking liberation from his tyranny. Evidence of more of Saddam's repression over the following years alienated some antiwar sympathizers. They might otherwise have supported protests against U.S. bombing of Iraqi military installations in and near the no-fly zone as an illegal use of force against a nation with which we were not at war.

But on September 11, 2001, a major shift in attention away from Iraq took place. Attacks involving hijacked airliners by nineteen members of the terrorist organization al-Qaeda destroyed the twin towers of the World Trade Center in New York, as well as parts of the Pentagon near Washington. About three thousand people were

*In 1991 an Iraqi family walks through the rubble of Karbala, a city in central Iraq where Saddam's forces had put down a Shiite rebellion.*

killed. The nation had experienced terrorist acts before but never of this magnitude. Americans were stunned, and a widespread sense of vulnerability resulted.

## "GRIEF NOT A CRY FOR WAR"

On the day of the terrorist attack, President George W. Bush promised the nation that "the United States will hunt down and punish those responsible for these cowardly acts." Al-Qaeda was operating training camps in Afghanistan. The U.S. government issued an ultimatum to Afghanistan's repressive Taliban rulers that they must close the camps and turn over al-Qaeda leader Osama bin Laden and his top lieutenants to U.S. authorities or face military action. Within a week of 9/11, peace

*After 9/11, the U.S. government sent the U.S. Marines into Afghanistan to stamp out al-Qaeda and the Taliban.*

groups were organizing to prevent the bombing of civilians in Afghanistan. In New York City, which had borne the brunt of the 9/11 attack, twenty-four-hour peace vigils were being held in Union Square. A sticker slogan eloquently expressed the sentiments of these New York activists. "Our Grief Is Not a Cry for War." Roughly two thousand people followed these vigils with a peaceful march to Times Square.

On October 7, President Bush told the nation that "U.S. forces have begun strikes on terrorist camps of al-Qaeda and the military installations of the Taliban regime in Afghanistan." A month later, students opposed to military action in Afghanistan gathered at regional peace conferences at Boston University, Georgia State University, George Washington University in Washington, D.C., Chicago's DePaul University, and the University of California at Berkeley.

Nevertheless, on campus and throughout the peace movement, reservations persisted. U.S. military action seemed to be ridding

Afghanistan of its tyrannical Taliban regime. Antiwar proponents were torn between rejecting violence and embracing the hope that violence would release Afghanistan women from the severe repression under which they had been living. Many resolved their doubts over the following months as the Taliban began regaining power and once again repressing women.

## WEAPONS OF MASS DESTRUCTION

In his January 2002 State of the Union address, President Bush singled out Iraq, along with Iran and North Korea, as part of the "axis of evil arming to threaten the peace of the world." He warned that "the United States of America will not permit the world's most dangerous regimes to threaten us with the world's most destructive weapons."

During the following months, Iraqi air defenses fired at U.S. jets patrolling the no-fly zone. Americans were told that their government had information that Iraq was developing both atomic weapons and a chemical-biological warfare program. President Bush and his advisers threatened military action to depose Saddam Hussein and effect a regime change in Iraq. When the United Nations demanded that Iraq allow the weapons inspectors it had previously expelled to return, Saddam's government at first refused.

Finally, in early September 2002, Iraq agreed to let inspections resume. Hans Blix of Sweden was reassigned to head the team of inspectors. The Bush administration's attitude toward renewing inspections was skeptical. Secretary of State Colin Powell pointed out that "we have seen this game [inspections] before."

Many Democrats and many in the peace movement questioned the claim that Iraq was developing weapons of mass destruction (WMDs). The White House denied requests for proof on the grounds that providing it would compromise intelligence sources and endanger national security. Fear that the government was laying the groundwork for war grew in the peace movement.

*UN inspectors went into Iraq in the fall of 2002 to look for WMDs.*

## A NEW ANGLE

By autumn 2002, a new phenomenon—the Internet—had emerged to recruit the forces of peace. Huge numbers of people from all around the world were able to contact each other quickly and share information from a great variety of sources. Many alternative media sources were available over the Internet. Among the most active were CommonDreams.org and MoveOn.org.

MoveOn.org had been started as an Internet website in 1998 to fight against the impeachment of President Bill Clinton. Another website operator, twenty-two-year-old Eli Pariser, had merged with MoveOn.org in 2001 and was soon directing a worldwide movement to enlist members against starting a war in Iraq. By October, MoveOn.org was claiming nine hundred thousand U.S. members. Other peace groups were also active. The American Friends Service Committee was part of a coalition sponsoring a peace pledge petition. Swarthmore College's Brandywine Peace Community was circulating a pledge of resistance for people who "will engage in civil disobedience and will nonviolently resist" waging war against Iraq. Other effective national organizing networks against war in Iraq included United for Peace and Justice, Act Now to Stop War and End Racism (ANSWER), Not in Our Name, and Win without War.

The leading political spokesperson for peace at this time was Democratic senator Robert Byrd of West Virginia. When President Bush, who had initially claimed he didn't need congressional approval to wage war in Iraq, decided to seek it anyway, eighty-four-year-old Senator Byrd opposed him. Day after day, he spoke out in the Senate, often to a largely empty chamber, in opposition to granting President Bush powers to wage war in Iraq. "We must not make the mistake of looking at the resolution before us as just another offshoot of the war on terror," he pointed out, his voice resounding but sometimes quavering. His hands shaking as he consulted his notes, he pointed out that,

*Senator Robert Byrd, the oldest member of the U.S. Congress, rose on March 19, 2003, to denounce as misguided President Bush's march to war with Iraq.*

"we are rushing into war without fully discussing why, without thoroughly considering the consequences, or without making any attempt to explore what steps we might take to avert a conflict." When Senator Byrd attempted a filibuster, the Senate chamber ended it by a vote of 95 to 1. On October 11, 2002, the Senate voted 77 to 23 to grant the president the war powers he wanted. Senator Byrd asked his supporters to urge the president "to heed the Constitution," whose values, Byrd said, "do not include using our position as the most formidable nation in the world to bully and intimidate other nations."

Representative Charles Rangel of New York City had also opposed granting war powers to President Bush. "When you talk about a war," he said, "you're talking about ground troops, you're talking about enlisted people, and they don't come from the kids and members of Congress." Some weeks later, he introduced a bill to reinstate the draft. He reminded prowar legislators and the administration that, during the Vietnam War, those who could afford to go to college were exempt from service while those who couldn't were drafted. He added, "for those who say the poor fight better, I say give the rich a chance." Defense Secretary Donald Rumsfeld flatly rejected the idea. "There is no need for it at all," he insisted.

## A ROAD TO WAR

As the peace movement grew and to some extent came together over the next few months, a road-to-war scenario played itself out. Initial reports by Hans Blix's UN inspection team were mixed. They asked for more time but cast doubts on the extent to which Iraq was cooperating. President Bush and Secretary of State Colin Powell said Iraq was stalling and this was part of a pattern of noncompliance with the terms of the 1991 peace agreement. The administration continued to claim it had conclusive evidence that Saddam was developing WMDs. The British offered proof of this, but the proof was later shown to be fraudulent.

Meanwhile, the Bush administration was attempting to build a coalition of forces to invade Iraq. France, Germany, Russia, and China were all in opposition. In countries such as Britain, Australia, Spain, and Italy, whose governments backed the U.S. position, their citizens voiced overwhelming opposition. UN approval of a U.S. invasion seemed increasingly unlikely. Nevertheless, U.S. armed forces were massing in Kuwait and other regions of the Gulf.

## MOUNTING PROTESTS

In January 2003, a full-page ad ran in the *Wall Street Journal*. It offered a "Dissent on Iraq" that prominent Republicans and GOP contributors, including retired high-ranking military officers and business leaders, had signed. Sociologist and author Todd Gitlin noted that the building movement against war with Iraq was "fairly mainstream— unions and churches, for example." A variety of antiwar actions took place. These included online petition drives, letter writing, and phone banks urging calls to the White House. Teach-ins occurred on campuses and in churches, and protesters blocked traffic at intersections and federal buildings in some cities. United for Peace and Justice, a coalition of seventy antiwar groups, acted as a networking resource to help organize more than 150 rallies in different locations across the country. It provided crucial antiwar action information to many grassroots movements and thousands of concerned individuals.

Thirty members of a self-declared Iraq Peace Team traveled to Iraq to stand alongside women and children when bombing took place. One of them, Cynthia Banas, a retired librarian from Vernon, New York, defined their mission: "If you can risk your life in a war [as a soldier], why can't you risk your life for peace?" she asked. On January 18, tens of thousands of people gathered in Washington, braving bone-chilling weather for hours, to oppose an invasion of Iraq. Their antiwar chants were echoed by peace rallies in major cities and small towns around the world.

Less than a month later, antiwar activists filed a lawsuit in federal court in Boston that sought to prevent President Bush from going to war against Iraq without congressional approval. The suit argued that the October resolution passed by Congress that gave him the power to attack Iraq was unconstitutional. The coalition bringing the action included six members of the House of Representatives, as well as several U.S. soldiers and parents of military personnel. A *New York Times*/CBS News poll taken at this time found that 59 percent of Americans believed the president should give UN inspectors more time. Another 63 percent said the United States should not act without support from its allies. And 56 percent said President Bush should wait for UN approval before launching an attack on Iraq.

From France to Australia, from the Philippines to Iceland, massive antiwar protests took place. They happened in every major U.S. city and involved a million or more Americans. In Detroit, Chicago, and Pittsburgh, in freezing weather, thousands rallied against the war. Demonstrations were held in small cities like Spencer, West Virginia, and Meadville, Pennsylvania, and Youngstown, Ohio. Tens of thousands protested in San Francisco and Los Angeles and smaller cities throughout California.

In New York City, antiwar organizers had been denied a permit to march to the United Nations for a rally on February 15. Police erected steel-barricaded pens up the length of First Avenue several blocks north of the UN building. As the pens filled up, police barricaded the blocks leading into the avenue, forcing protesters to walk farther and farther north of the UN. As many as half a million demonstrators clogged the side streets and adjacent thoroughfares and caused the police to shut down the Fifty-Ninth Street Bridge. The police hoped to prevent additional protesters from joining the mass of people tying up traffic on the east side of Manhattan Island. Frustrated protesters clashed with mounted police, and two hundred people were arrested. Among those trapped in the chaos were a group of relatives of people killed on 9/11. Catherine Montano, whose son

*Antiwar protesters demonstrated near UN headquarters on February 15, 2003, in New York to protest a possible U.S.-led attack on Iraq. The crowd, which stretched for twenty blocks along First Avenue, was part of a global protest.*

was a 9/11 victim, explained their presence: "We cannot have wars in this day and age," she said. "If my son were alive he would have been here too."

## NOT A JUST WAR

In early March, the Turkish parliament voted not to allow U.S. troops to set up bases on the Iraqi border. That meant a complete change of plans for the invasion of Iraq. This vote raised hopes of the invasion being postponed or perhaps even canceled. Hopes were raised further a few days later when Mohamed El Baradei, director general of the International Atomic Energy Agency (IAEA), told the UN Security Council that documents supporting U.S. claims that Iraq was buying materials used for uranium enrichment in construction of nuclear weapons were forgeries. El Baradei reported finding no evidence of banned weapons or nuclear material in Iraq. However, the Bush administration stood by its claims that Saddam was developing WMDs.

On March 9, former president Jimmy Carter, who had recently been awarded the Nobel Peace Prize, wrote in the *New York Times* that a unilateral attack by the United States on Iraq would not meet the criteria of a just war. He wrote that "American stature will surely decline further if we launch a war in clear defiance of the United Nations." It would violate "basic religious principles" and "respect for international law." Opposition to the war based on religious principles also was declared by the pope, the Catholic Bishops of America, and the National Council of Churches.

In the United Nations, attempts by the United States and its ally Great Britain to push through a resolution authorizing war against Iraq were thwarted when France and Russia vowed to veto it. UN secretary general Kofi Annan warned Washington that, without UN authorization, an invasion would be illegitimate. President Bush insisted that he had the legal authority to attack Iraq. On March 18, he warned Saddam Hussein that if he didn't abdicate, U.S. forces would attack "at a time of our choosing."

## AROUND THE WORLD PROTESTS

At 10:16 P.M. eastern standard time on Wednesday, March 19, 2003, President Bush announced that "early stages of military operations to disarm Iraq" had begun. Early the next morning, the first bombs of a two-day barrage fell on Baghdad. On the Senate floor, Senator Byrd lamented the attack. "No more is the image of America one of a strong yet benevolent peacekeeper," he declared.

As the war started, massive demonstrations took place against it, not just in the United States but also abroad. On March 20, between one hundred thousand and two hundred thousand people demonstrated in Athens, chanting "Bush—killer!" Other protests followed in Pakistan, Australia, Indonesia, Germany, Denmark, Switzerland, Spain, and Italy. In San Francisco, on March 21, when protesters blocked streets leading to the Oakland Bay Bridge and clashed with police, over one thousand people were arrested. Large protests also happened in Boston and New York.

On March 22, the media reported a march in New York City that was "20 abreast and 40 blocks long." Organized by the coalition United for Peace and Justice, the crowd was estimated at two hundred thousand people. When about half of them reached Washington Square, the police tried to disperse them. Other protesters were still pouring in, and scuffles broke out. The police used their billy clubs, and arrests were made. Rally organizers protested that the police had exceeded their authority.

The next day, approximately six hundred people gathered at Times Square waving American flags and chanting "U-S-A! U-S-A!"

*More than fifty thousand antiwar protesters gathered in Berlin, Germany, in March 2003 to demonstrate against the U.S.-led war in Iraq.*

in support of the war. In Richmond, Virginia, more than five thousand pro-war supporters gathered. Clear Channel Communications, the largest radio broadcast corporation in the United States, had sponsored pro-war rallies complete with complimentary American flags. However, while many demonstrations of support for the war took place across the country, the numbers did not approach those of the antiwar rallies.

## CELEBRITY FLAPS

Among those who spoke out against the war were several movie celebrities. These included Barbra Streisand, Ed Asner, Susan Sarandon, Sean Penn, and other stars. Rumors abounded of an unofficial blacklist of antiwar actors who were vocal. It was even whispered that Sean Penn's name might be on it. In fact, no proof existed of any blacklist. Had there been, stars like Penn were undoubtedly too popular at the box office to be affected. Nevertheless, the rumors alone may have been enough to give lesser screen personalities second thoughts about making antiwar speeches.

The movie industry was nervous. The Academy Awards ceremony was scheduled for the week after Operation Iraqi Freedom began. Patriotism was running high, and there had been resentment voiced in the media against antiwar celebrities. It was decided that political speeches would be banned from the Oscar ceremonies.

When controversial filmmaker Michael Moore won the award for Best Documentary, he accepted the Oscar wearing a badge reading "Shoot movies, not Iraqis." In his acceptance speech, he said, "We are against this war, Mr. Bush. Shame on you, Mr. Bush." He was both booed and applauded, a reaction that may have reflected the split in the country over the war.

A few weeks later, actor Tim Robbins received a letter from Dale Petroskey, the president of the Baseball Hall of Fame. Robbins and his partner, Susan Sarandon, had been invited to the Hall of Fame's fifteenth anniversary celebration of their popular hit movie, *Bull Durham*. The letter, which was also sent to the media, said that Robbins's public criticism of President Bush was undermining the U.S. position. The group felt this stance could put U.S. troops in even more danger. As a result, the program honoring *Bull Durham* had been canceled. Robbins wrote back to Petroskey that his action was "embarrassing to baseball," and concluded "long live democracy, free speech and the '69 Mets."

## THE BACKLASH

Two weeks into Operation Iraqi Freedom, the *Christian Science Monitor* reported a mounting backlash to the protests of the peace movement. American soldiers were fighting and dying on foreign soil. A growing feeling emerged that demonstrators were undercutting their efforts. Peace activists had always heard murmurs doubting their patriotism, but now they were being called traitors. Two-thirds of the country supported the war, according to various polls. Only a small percentage of the remaining one-third were actually active in the anti-war movement.

At first, there had been setbacks in Iraq, but, as the war continued, victory seemed increasingly close at hand. A large majority of Americans approved of President Bush's Iraq policies. A wellspring of patriotic pride isolated dissenters. Although they insisted that they supported the troops and chanted "Bring them home!" the message wasn't getting across. As·one soldier put it, "If they are not backing up those that are in charge of *us,* then in the long run, they're not backing *us* up."

On May 1, 2003, in a nationally televised ceremony from the flight deck of the aircraft carrier USS *Abraham Lincoln*, President Bush announced that combat operations had ended in Iraq. The statement, however, proved to be premature. Just six weeks later, the United States launched Operation Desert Scorpion, which focused fighting mainly in the Iraqi town of Fallujah against Iraqi insurgents and supporters of Saddam. The war, it seemed, would not be finished as quickly as supporters once believed.

On December 14, 2003, U.S. troops found Saddam hiding in a hole near his hometown of Tikrit. Images of his capture appeared all over the world, and many supporters of the war saw this as proof of the war's success. Many people saw the removal of the Iraqi tyrant as cause for celebration. But, as Saddam's supporters reorganized to retaliate, Iraq experienced ongoing instability.

March 20, 2004, marked the one-year anniversary of the war in Iraq. Large antiwar protests took place in towns and cities throughout the world. In the United States, antiwar groups sponsored marches and rallies from Montpelier, Vermont, to Crawford, Texas (where President Bush's ranch is located), to Los Angeles, California. In Los Angeles, protesters lined up a pair of shoes for every soldier killed during the war in Iraq. The number at the time was 560. Almost a year later, that number had risen to 1,437.

The peace movement spread in January 2005, when the government announced

*In 2004 pairs of boots in Los Angeles represent soldiers killed in Iraq.*

that it was ending its search for WMDs. Americans who once supported the war were suddenly questioning its validity. Although WMDs were never found, the U.S. military remained in Iraq to help the country create its own government. With the help of UN officials, Iraq put together an electoral system and held a countrywide election.

Some Americans who saw the pictures of Iraqi citizens leaving the voting polls felt proud of the United States for assisting in bringing about governmental change. Others, like those in the peace movement, continued to feel that every life lost was an enormous price to pay for a war that they believed was unnecessary. As the second anniversary of the war approached, organizations for peace once again gathered together to demonstrate for peace. As they have done in protests past, these peace demonstrators mourned the dead, advocated for the living, and looked toward the future.

***T*he real and lasting victories
are those of peace, and not of war.**
—*Ralph Waldo Emerson, 1860*

# AFTERWORD

In the aftermath of war, the question is often asked: Was it worth it? The destruction, the loss of life and limb, the heartbreak and inhumanity—was it worth it? Even when right is on our side, is there not a better way than violence, the shedding of blood, the taking of life? Even when the cause is humane, the ends just, is there not a better way? Those who are active in the cause of peace believe that there must be.

Others raise powerful arguments against them. Without war and bloodshed, they say, the United States would not have become a country, slavery might never have been ended, Hitler's horrors might still prevail. When attacked we must defend ourselves. When threatened with attack, we must act before it is too late. Evil must not be allowed to spread over the world. When humans are oppressed, our humanity demands that we come to their aid.

Yes, but are we willing that our children should die for such causes? When it is our loved one in the body bag, what then? When poor boys fight and die while rich boys go to college, when arms dealers profit while bombs fall on innocent children, when atrocities are committed to revenge enemy atrocities, what then? When decent young men and women are dehumanized into killers in the name of humanity, what then? These are the questions raised by activists for peace.

Yes, but people may dream of peace, yet realities must be faced. Oppressed people rise up and fight for their freedom. Some Americans argue that it is necessary to come to their aid. They argue that to close one's eyes to evil and to refuse to act against it is unworthy of our traditions. There may be injustices in war, but not all wars are unjust. Honor, duty, loyalty—these are American values worth fighting for, insist those whose patriotism does not balk at the horrors of war.

The choice remains. Should we turn the other cheek or stand up and fight? Should we seek alternatives to violence or wage war for our principles? Is the dream of everlasting peace just that, only a dream? Antiwar activists believe it is more than that.

# TIMELINE

**1776** Colonists persecute Quakers, Mennonites, and Brethren for refusing to fight in the American Revolution.

**1828** William Ladd founds the American Peace Society (APS).

**1838** The APS splits over accepting women as members. A splinter group—the New England Non-Resistant Society—forms.

**1846** Henry David Thoreau is jailed for refusing to pay state taxes that support the Mexican-American War.

**1863–1864** Secret antiwar societies are formed in the Confederacy.

**1866** The Universal Peace Union (UPU) is founded, with Alfred Love as president. It calls for the immediate disarmament of all nations.

**1892** The International Peace Bureau is founded.

**1898** Politicians and industrialists found the Anti-Imperialist League (A-IL).

**1899** The first Hague Peace Conference meets.

**1904** Three thousand people, representing nearly two hundred peace organizations, attend the Boston Peace Congress.

**1906** Andrew Carnegie organizes the New York Peace Society (NYPS).

**1907** NYPS organizes the first National Peace Congress, which twenty-seven millionaires attend. The second Hague Peace Conference is held.

**1910** Carnegie launches the Carnegie Endowment for International Peace.

**1912** The NYPS merges with the APS.

**1915** Woman's Peace Party is formed.

**1917** In the U.S. Congress, Jeannette Rankin votes against U.S. entry into World War I.

**1919** Women's Peace Society (WPS) is formed.

**1928** The United States signs the Kellogg-Briand Pact renouncing war.

**1935–1936** The Neutrality Act becomes law and is expanded.

**1939** Republican isolationists form the America First Committee to oppose any military build-up that would lead to U.S. involvement in a war.

**1941** Jeannette Rankin casts the only vote against declaring war on Japan.

**1950–1953** Two million Americans sign the Stockholm Peace Appeal circulated by the World Peace Council.

**1957** The National Committee for a Sane Nuclear Policy (SANE) is formed.

**1966–1967** Mass anti–Vietnam War marches take place in many U.S. cities.

**1968** Antiwar students occupy five buildings at Columbia University in New York. In Chicago, antiwar protesters hold rallies during the Democratic National Convention.

**1970** Police kill six college students in Ohio and Mississippi during protests against the U.S. invasion of Cambodia.

**1971** At a huge antiwar rally in Washington, D.C., seven hundred Vietnam veterans discard their medals.

**1983** Roman Catholic bishops urge Catholics to oppose the nuclear arms race.

**1984** The U.S. Congress sets up the U.S. Institute of Peace.

**1991** Protests against the first Gulf War take place in the United States.

**2002** MoveOn.org enlists nearly a million members against starting a war in Iraq. Senator Robert Byrd speaks against giving President Bush the power to wage war in Iraq.

**2003** Around the country, millions gather at antiwar rallies to protest the second war against Iraq.

**2004** On the second anniversary of the war, large antiwar rallies take place throughout the world.

**2005** The peace movement spreads after the U.S. government ends its search for weapons of mass destruction in Iraq and finds none.

# SOURCE NOTES

2 Mary Heaton Vorse, *A Footnote to Folly: Reminiscences of Mary Heaton Vorse* (1935, reprint, New York: Arno Press, 1980), 85.

8 Thomas D. Hamm, *The Quakers of America* (New York: Columbia University Press, 2003), 25.

10 *Encyclopaedia Britannica,* 15th edition, Vol. 7, 817.

13 "Religion and the American Revolution" *Library of Congress,* n.d., http://www.loc. gov/exhibits/religion/re103.html (March 2, 2005).

15 *MCC Mission Statement from the Mennonite Central Committee,* n.d., http://www.mcc.org/peacecommit.html (March 2, 2005).

15 *Encyclopaedia Britannica,* 15th edition, Vol. 11, 904.

17 *MCC Mission Statement.*

18 "The Convention of the Delegates of Eighteen Counties of Virginia, Held at Staunton, on the 21st of September, for the Purpose of Forming a General Ticket of Electors of President and Vice-President, to the Freeholders of Virginia," *Library of Congress,* n.d. http://memory .loc.gov/cgibin/query/r?ammem/rbpe:@ field(DOCID+@lit(rbpe18301200)) (February 11, 2005).

19 Duncan Rea Williams III, *Quakers and the Indians,* n.d., http://www.drwilliams .org/iDoc/Web-213.htm (March 3, 2005).

19 Howard Zinn, *A People's History of the United States* (New York: Harper & Row, 1980), 124.

19 Samuel Elliot Morison, *The Oxford History of the American People* (New York: Oxford University Press, 1965), 381.

21 Peter Rinaldo, *Unnecessary Wars: Causes and Effects of United States Wars from the American Revolution to Vietnam* (Briarcliff Manor, NY: DorPete Press, 1993), 15.

22 *The War of 1812: Impressment,* n.d., www.galafilm.com/1812/e/background/ brit_impress.html (March 3, 2005).

23 Rinaldo, 16.

23 Charles A. Beard and Mary R. Beard, *The Rise of American Civilization,* Vol. 1 (New York: Macmillan, 1939), 410.

24 Henry Steele Commager, *Documents of American History,* Vol. 1 (Englewood Cliffs, NJ: Prentice Hall, 1973), 207–209.

24 *Encyclopaedia Britannica,* 15th edition, Vol. 10, 550.

25 *The War of 1812: Antiwar Movement,* n.d., http://www.galafilm.com/1812/e/ background/amer_antiwar.html (March 3, 2005).

26 *U.S. History.com: War of 1812 Hartford Convention,* n.d., http:// www.u-s history .com/pages/h512.html (March 3, 2005).

26 William Miller, *A New History of the United States* (New York: George Brazilier, 1958), 156.

26 Ibid.

26 Ibid.

28 Marty Jezer, *The Power of the People.* eds. by Robert Cooney and Helen Michalowski (Philadelphia: New Society Publishers, 1987), 25.

28 *Encyclopaedia Britannica,* 15th edition, Vol. 2, 738.

29 Harriet Hyman Alonso, *The Women's Peace Union and the Outlawry of War, 1921–1942* (Knoxville: The University of Tennessee Press, 1989), 3.

30 Ibid.

30 *Encyclopaedia Britannica,* 15th edition, Vol. 7, 574.

32 Ibid.

32 Merle Curti, *Peace or War: The American Struggle, 1636–1936* (New York: W. W. Norton & Company, 1936), 45.

33 Zinn, 148–149.

33 James M. McPherson, *The Battle Cry of Freedom: The Civil War Era* (New York: Oxford University Press, 1988), 51.

33 Alonso, 6.

34 Zinn, 151.

34 Ibid.

34 Milton Meltzer and Walter Harding, *A Thoreau Profile* (Lincoln, MA.: The Thoreau Society, 1998), 163.

35 Ibid., 161–162.

35 Henry David Thoreau. *Walden and Civil Disobedience* (New York: Penguin Books, 1986), 362.

36 William W. Holden, "The Memoirs of William W. Holden," *Documenting the American South,* n.d., http://docsouth .unc.edu/holden/menu.html (February 14, 2005).

37 Meltzer and Harding, 261.

37 Ibid., 267.

38 Curti, 47.

38 Ibid., 54.

38 McPherson, 204.

39 Curti, 54.

39 McPherson, 596.

40 Ibid., 597.

42 Herbert Asbury, *The Gangs of New York: An Informal History of the Underworld* (New York: Thunder's Mouth Press, 1998), 112, 117.

43 Ibid., 125.

44 McPherson, 613.

45 Ibid., 696.

45 Ibid., 695.

46 Ibid., 854.

47 Curti, 77.

48 Ibid., 79.

48 Ibid., 170.

49 Stanley Karnow, *In Our Image: America's Empire in the Philippines* (New York: Random House, 1989), 89.

49 Philip Knightley, *The First Casualty* (New York: Harcourt Brace Jovanovich, 1975), 55.

50 Miller, 331.

51 Knightley, 56.

51 Miller, 331.

51 Curti, 168.

51 Karnow, 101.

52 Ibid., 109.

52 Ibid., 124.

52 Ibid., 114.

52 "The Anti-Imperialist League 1898–1902" *The American Peace Movements,* n.d., http://www.culture-of-peace.info/ apm/chapter1-3.html (March 3, 2005).

52 Ibid.

52 Karnow, 110.

52 Zinn, 307.

53 Miller, 334.

56 Alfred Bryan, "I Didn't Raise My Boy to Be a Soldier," *USGENNET,* n.d., http:// www.usgennet.org/usa/mo/county/ stlouis/ww1-music/nosoldier.htm (March 3, 2005).

58 Barbara W. Tuchman, *The Proud Tower* (New York: Bantam Books, 1967), 268.

58 Ibid., 525.

59 Anne Commire and Deborah Klezmer, "Karl Marx" *Historic World Leaders* (Detroit: Gale Research, Inc., 1994), 4.

59 Tuchman, 525.

59 "The Anti-Imperialist League 1898–1902."

63 Clifton Daniel, ed., *Chronicle of the 20th Century* (Mount Kisco, NY: Chronicle Publications, 1987), 217.

63 Zinn, 352.

63 Ibid., 355.

63 "The People's Council of America 1917–1919," *The American Peace Movements,* n.d., http://www.culture-of-peace.info/apm/ chapter2-5.html (March 3, 2005).

64 Ibid.

64 Elder Witt, ed., *The Supreme Court and Individual Rights* (Washington, DC: Congressional Quarterly, Inc., 1980), 24–25.

64 Ibid., 25.

65 Ibid., 24.

65 "Goldstein V. United States 258 Fed. 908," *The Star-Spangled Banner,* n.d., http://www.geocities.com/irby.geo/fsk.html (March 3, 2005).

66 Zinn, 355.

66 Ibid.

66 Tuchman, 525.

67 Zinn, 360.

68 Kevin S. Giles, *Flight of the Dove: The Story of Jeannette Rankin* (Beaverton, OR: Touchstone Press, 1980), 14.

69 Alonso, 9.

69 Ibid., 2–13.

69 "The People's Council of America 1917–1919."

73 "Anna B. Eckstein Papers, 1886–1944," *Swarthmore College Peace Collection,* n.d., www.swarthmore.edu/Library/peace/CDGB/eckstein.htm (March 3, 2005).

74 *Encyclopaedia Britannica,* 15th edition, Vol. 5, 751.

74 Ted Gottfried, *Eleanor Roosevelt: First Lady of the 20th Century* (New York: Franklin Watts, 1997), 69.

76 *Behind the Headlines,* n.d., http://www.antiwar.com/justin/j101599.html (March 3, 2005).

76 Curti, 285.

77 Guenter Lewy, *Peace & Revolution: The Moral Crisis of American Pacifism* (Grand Rapids, MI: William B. Eerdmans Publishing Company, 1988), 6.

77 Ibid., 8.

78 David Adams, "The American League Against War and Fascism and the Emergency Peace Campaign 1933–1939" *The American Peace Movements,* n.d., http://www.culture-of-peace.info/apm/chapter3-8.html (March 3, 2005).

78 Ibid.

79 Daniel, 498.

81 Alonso, 160.

81 Miller, 385.

81 *Encyclopaedia Britannica,* 15th edition, Vol. 6, 140.

81 David McCullough, *Truman* (New York: Simon & Schuster, 1992), 254.

81 Daniel, 531.

88 Ibid., 963.

89 Mike Gravel, ed., *The Pentagon Papers,* vol. 1, (Boston: Beacon Press, 1971), 241.

89 Nikita Khrushchev, "Statement at the Polish Embassy, Moscow, 1956," *Bartlett's Familiar Quotations,* 14th ed. (Boston: Little Brown and Company, 1968), 1032B.

90 Zinn, 462.

91 Daniel, 941.

92 Ibid., 971.

93 Jessica Mitford, *The Trial of Dr. Spock* (New York: Alfred A. Knopf, 1969), 4–5.

93 Daniel, 983.

95 Ibid., 980.

96 Ibid., 987.

96 James Miller, *Democracy Is in the Streets* (New York: Simon & Schuster, 1987), 395.

97 Ibid., 299.

99 Ibid., 297.

99 Ibid., 304.

99 Daniel, 1020.

103 Ibid., 1219.

106 Ramsey Clark, *The Fire This Time: U.S. War Crimes in the Gulf* (New York: Thunder's Mouth Press, 1992), xvi.

107 "September 11: Chronology of Terror," *CNN.com,* n.d., http://www.cnn.com/2001/US/09/11/chronology.attack (March 3, 2005).

108 Ian Christopher McCaleb, "Bush Announces Opening of Attacks," *CNN.com,* n.d., http://www.cnn.com/2001/US/10/07/ret.attack.Bush/index.html (March 3, 2005).

109 George W. Bush, "President Delivers State of the Union Address," *The White House,* news release, January 29, 2002, http://www.whitehouse.gov/news/releases/2002/01/20020129-11.html (March 3, 2005).

109 "Weapons Inspectors Meet with Iraq," *CNN.com/WORLD,* December 17, 2002, http://www.cnn.com/2002/WORLD/meast/09/17/iraq.un (March 3, 2005).

111 Eils Lotozo, "Making a Case for Peace," *Philadelphia Inquirer,* September 24, 2002, http://www.philly.com/mld/inquirer/living/people/4137314.htm (March 3, 2005).

112 Robert Byrd, "Excerpt of Speeches Made on Senate Floor," *New York Times,* October 4, 2002, http://www.nytimes.com/2002/10/04/politics/04ITEX.html (March 3, 2005).

112 Paul J. Nyden, "Byrd Pleads to American People," *Charleston Gazette,* October 11, 2002, http://www.flagstaffactivist.org/war/byrd101102.html (March 3, 2005).

112 "Rangel Calls for Mandatory Military Service," *CNN.com/Inside Politics,* December 30, 2002, http://www.cnn.com/2002/ALLPOLITICS/12/29/mandatory.military (March 3, 2005).

112 "Rangel Introduces Bill to Reinstate Draft," *CNN.com/Inside Politics,* January 8, 2003, http://www.cnn.com/2003/ALLPOLITICS/01/07/rangel.draft (March 3, 2005).

112 Ibid.

113 Frank Davies, "Anti-War Activists Say They Are Just Starting to Find Voice," *Miami Herald,* January 18, 2003, 1.

113 Scott Peterson, "Few But Proud: US Antiwar Activists in Iraq," *Christian Science Monitor,* December 17, 2002, 1.

115 Bill Vann, "Massive New York City Rally Spills into Streets," *World Socialist Website,* February 17, 2003, http://www.wsws.org/articles/2003/feb2003/nyc-f17.shtml (March 3, 2005).

116 "Carter Warns about War on Iraq," *Associated Press,* March 9, 2003, http://www.endthewar.org/features/carter1.htm (March 3, 2005).

116 Paul Eastham and William Lowther, "Bush Warns Saddam: Go in 48 Hours or We Invade," *Daily Mail,* March 18, 2003, 1.

116 George W. Bush, "Remarks by the President in Address to the Nation," *The White House,* news release, March 19, 2003, http://www.usinfo.state.gov/regional/nea/iraq/text2003/0319bush.htm (March 3, 2005).

116 "War Begins with Air Strikes, Bush Addresses Nation," *WPXI.com,* March 20, 2003, http://www.wpxi.com/iraq/2052725/detail.html (March 3, 2005).

117 Michael Powell, "Around Globe, Protest Marches," *Washington Post,* March 23, 2003, A19 (March 3, 2005).

118 Kevin Willman, "Highs and Lows of Oscar Ceremonies," *ChronWatch,* March 27, 2003, http://www.chronwatch.com/content/contentDisplay.asp?aid=2067&catcode=11 (March 3, 2005).

119 Tim Robbins, "Tim Robbins vs. the Baseball Hall of Fame," *Nation and Common Dreams News Center,* May 21, 2003, http://www.commondreams.org/views03/0412-09.htm (March 3, 2005).

119 Kim Campbell, Alexandra Marks, and Ben Arnoldy, "Antiwar Protesters in a PR Fix," *Christian Science Monitor,* April 2, 2003, 1.

122 Ralph Waldo Emerson, "Conduct of Life: Worship," *The Works of Ralph Waldo Emerson,* February 5, 2005, http://www.rwe.org/works/Conduct_6_Worship.htm (March 2, 2005).

# SELECTED BIBLIOGRAPHY

Asbury, Herbert. *The Gangs of New York: An Informal History of the Underworld.* New York: Thunder's Mouth Press, 1998.

Beard, Charles A., and Mary R. Beard. *The Rise of American Civilization.* Vol 1. New York: MacMillan, 1939.

Clark, Ramsey. *The Fire This Time: U.S. War Crimes in the Gulf.* New York: Thunder's Mouth Press, 1992.

Commauger, Henry Steele. *Documents of American History,* Vol. 1. Englewood Cliffs, NJ: Prentice Hall, 1973.

Curti, Merle. *Peace or War: The American Struggle (1636–1936).* New York: W. W. Norton & Company, 1936.

Daniel, Clifon, ed. *Chronicle of the 20th Century.* Mount Kisco, NY: Chronicle Publications, 1987.

De Latil, Pierre. *Enrico Fermi: The Man and His Theories.* New York: Paul S. Eriksson, 1966.

Gottfried, Ted. *Eleanor Roosevelt: First Lady of the 20th Century.* New York: Franklin Watts, 1997.

Gravel, Mike, ed. *The Pentagon Papers.* Vol. 1. Boston: Beacon Press, 1971.

Halberstram, David. *The Fifties.* New York: Villard Books, 1983.

Karnow, Stanley. *In Our Image: America's Empire in the Philippines.* New York: Random House, 1989.

———. *Vietnam: A History.* New York: The Viking Press, 1983.

Knightley, Philip. *The First Casualty.* New York: Harcourt Brace Jovanovich, 1975.

Lewy, Guenter. *Peace & Revolution: The Moral Crisis of American Pacifism.* Grand Rapids, MI: William B. Eerdmans Publishing Company, 1988.

Maier, Thomas. *Dr. Spock: An American Life*. New York: Harcourt Brace & Company, 1998.

McCullough, David. *Truman*. New York: Simon & Schuster, 1992.

McPherson, James M. *The Battle Cry of Freedom: The Civil War Era*. New York: Oxford University Press, 1988.

Mee, Charles L. Jr. *Meeting at Potsdam*. New York: M. Evans & Company, 1975.

Meltzer, Milton, and Walter Harding. *A Thoreau Profile*. Lincoln, MA: The Thoreau Society, 1998.

Miller, James. *Democracy Is in the Streets*. New York: Simon & Schuster, 1987.

Miller, William. *A New History of the United States*. New York: George Brazilier, 1958.

Mitford, Jessica. *The Trial of Dr. Spock*. New York: Alfred A. Knopf, 1969.

Morison, Samuel Elliot. *The Oxford History of the American People*. New York: Oxford University Press, 1965.

Rhodes, Richard. *The Making of the Atomic Bomb*. New York: Simon & Schuster, 1986.

Rinaldo, Peter. *Unnecessary Wars: Causes and Effects of United States Wars from the American Revolution to Vietnam*. Briarcliff Manor, NY: DorPete Press, 1993.

Segre, Emilio. *Enrico Fermi: Physicist*. Chicago: University of Chicago Press, 1970.

Tuchman, Barbara W. *The Proud Tower*. New York: Bantam Books, 1967.

Witt, Elder, ed. *The Supreme Court and Individual Rights*. Washington, DC: Congressional Quarterly, Inc., 1980.

# FURTHER READING AND WEBSITES

Alsonso, Harriet Hyman. *The Women's Peace Union and the Outlawry of War, 1921–1942*. Knoxville, TN: The University of Tennessee Press, 1989.

Arnold, James. R, and Roberta Wiener. *Lost Cause: The Civil War at Home, 1861–1865*. Minneapolis: Lerner Publications Company, 2002.

Bohannon, Lisa Frederiksen. *The American Revolution*. Minneapolis: Lerner Publications Company, 2004.

*Fellowship of Reconciliation—Peace, Justice, and Nonviolence.* http://www.forusa.org. The Fellowship of Reconciliation is an interfaith group, providing educational programs to promote domestic and international peace. The U.S. fellowship is also a part of the forty-nation International Fellowship of Reconciliation.

Galt, Margo Fortunato. *Stop This War! American Protest of the Conflict in Vietnam*. Minneapolis: Lerner Publications Company, 2000.

Goldstein, Margaret J. *Irish in America*. Minneapolis: Lerner Publications Company, 2005.

Karnow, Stanley. *Vietnam: A History*. New York: The Viking Press, 1983.

Levy, Debbie. *The Vietnam War*. Minneapolis: Lerner Publications Company, 2004.

Manheimer, Ann S. *Martin Luther King Jr.: Dreaming of Equality*. Minneapolis: Carolrhoda Books, Inc., 2005.

Martin, Christopher. *Mohandas K. Gandhi*. Minneapolis: Lerner Publications Company, 2001.

McPherson, Stephanie Sammartino. *Peace and Bread. The Story of Jane Addams*. Minneapolis: Carolrhoda Books, Inc., 1993.

Miller, William. *A New History of the United States*. New York: George Barilier, 1958.

MoveOn.org. *MoveOn.org: Democracy in Action.* http://www.moveon. org. This online, nationwide network takes a grassroots approach to helping people become politically involved by organizing them into electronic advocacy groups.

NGO Committee on Disarmament. Peace and Security. http://disarm. igc.org. This nongovernmental organization (NGO) provides facilities for organizing conferences and publishing information on disarmament. It also is an ongoing liaison with the United Nations.

Peace Action. *Peace Action: Practical, Positive Alternatives for Peace.* http://www.peace-action.org. This group evolved from the merger of of SANE and The Freeze, both antinuclear groups, and continues to work for the global abolition of nuclear weapons.

Sherman, Josepha. *The Cold War.* Minneapolis: Lerner Publications Company, 2004.

United States Institute of Peace. *United States Institute of Peace: Committed to the Peaceful Resolution of International Conflict.* http://www.usip. org. Formed by the U.S. Congress in 1984, this nonpartisan federal institution provides grants, training, educational programs, and publications to promote the peaceful resolution of international conflicts.

Zinn, Howard. *Declarations of Independence.* New York: HarperCollins Publishers, 1990.

———. *A People's History of the United States.* New York: Harper & Row, 1980.

# INDEX

# PHOTO ACKNOWLEDGMENTS

**The images in this book are used with the permission of:** © AP/Wide World Photos, pp. 2, 62, 79, 82, 85, 93, 94, 95, 97, 102, 104, 115; © Todd Strand/Independent Picture Service, p. 6; © Bettmann/CORBIS, pp. 10, 80, 86, 87, 89, 101, 122; © Brown Brothers, pp. 12, 20, 22, 37, 40, 43, 60, 74, 83; Library of Congress, pp. 16 [LC-USZ62-9487], 27 [LC-USZ62-7831], 28 [LC-USZC4-5321], 31 [LC-USZ62-7722], 53, 54 [LC-USZ62-10291], 68 [LC-USZ62-75334]; The Library Company of Philadelphia, p. 18; New York Public Library Picture Collection, pp. 25, 29 (right), 35, 71; Swarthmore College Peace Collection, pp. 29 (left), 47, 50, 69, 73; National Archives [W&C 256], p. 36; Courtesy of the North Carolina Division of Archives and History, p. 45; U.S. Naval Historical Center Photograph, p. 46; © Underwood & Underwood/CORBIS, p. 56; © HultonArchive/Getty Images, p. 59, © MPI/Getty Images, pp. 66, 90; DN-0066470, Chicago Daily News negatives collection, Chicago Historical Society, p. 75; © John Filo/Getty Images, p. 100; © Shepard Sherbell/CORBIS SABA, p. 107; U.S. Marines, p. 108; © Ahmed al Rubayyh/Getty Images, p. 110; © Reuters/CORBIS, p. 111; © Kurt Vinion/Getty Images, p. 117; © ROBYN BECK/AFP/Getty Images, p. 120; © UPI/Corbis/Bettmann, p. 122.

Cover: © AP/Wide World Photos.

# TITLES FROM THE AWARD-WINNING PEOPLE'S HISTORY SERIES:

*Accept No Substitutes! The History of American Advertising*

*Declaring Independence: Life During the American Revolution*

*Don't Whistle in School: The History of America's Public Schools*

*Dressed for the Occasion: What Americans Wore 1620-1970*

*Failure Is Impossible! The History of American Women's Rights*

*The Fight for Peace: A History of Antiwar Movements in America*

*Good Women of a Well-Blessed Land: Women's Lives in Colonial America*

*Headin' for Better Times: The Arts of the Great Depression*

*Into the Land of Freedom: African Americans in Reconstruction*

*Journalists at Risk: Reporting America's Wars*

*Thar She Blows: American Whaling in the Nineteenth Century*

*We Shall Overcome: The History of the American Civil Rights Movement*

*What's Cooking? The History of American Food*